OUT OF LINE

GROWING UP SOVIET

TINA GRIMBERG

TUNDRA BOOKS

Published in Canada by Tundra Books,
75 Sherbourne Street, Toronto, Ontario M5A 2P9

Published in the United States by Tundra Books of Northern New York,
P.O. Box 1030, Plattsburgh, New York 12901

Library of Congress Control Number: 2007920591

Library and Archives Canada Cataloguing in Publication

Grimberg, Tina
Out of line : growing up Soviet / Tina Grimberg.

ISBN 978-0-88776-803-3

1. Grimberg, Tina–Childhood and youth–Juvenile literature. 2. Ukraine–Social conditions–1945-1991–Juvenile literature. 3. Jewish children–Ukraine–Kiev–Biography–Juvenile literature. 4. Kiev (Ukraine)–Biography–Juvenile literature. I. Title.

DK508.934.G75A3 2007 j947.7/7085092 C2007-900221-8

We acknowledge the financial support of the Government of Canada through the Book Publishing Industry Development Program (BPIDP) and that of the Government of Ontario through the Ontario Media Development Corporation's Ontario Book Initiative. We further acknowledge the support of the Canada Council for the Arts and the Ontario Arts Council for our publishing program.

ONTARIO ARTS COUNCIL
CONSEIL DES ARTS DE L'ONTARIO

Design: Jennifer Lum

Printed and bound in Canada

This book is printed on acid-free paper that is 100% recycled, ancient-forest friendly (40% post-consumer recycled).

1 2 3 4 5 6 12 11 10 09 08 07

This book is dedicated with love and admiration to my grandparents,
Ginda and David Grimberg and Bronya and Misha Peker.
Zichronam livracha – *may their memory be blessed.*

CONTENTS

PREFACE

For over seventy years, much of the world was divided into two parts – East and West – or the communist block and the free world. The people within those parts feared each other. Millions of words were written about the differences between them and the evils of their ways. There were times when those differences brought the world to the brink of nuclear disaster. Looking back now, what amazes me is how little we actually knew about one another.

I grew up in Kiev, the capital city of Ukraine in the Soviet Union, often referred to globally as Russia. In the 1970s, the Soviet Union agreed to allow certain "undesirables" (Jews and some minorities) to leave Russia. I was fifteen the year that my parents made the decision to leave, and eventually we were sponsored by kind strangers in Indiana, who helped us settle in the United States. You can't visit Soviet Ukraine where I grew up. It doesn't exist anymore. The Soviet Union was disbanded in 1989.

For better or worse, I was formed by the communist world. This book is about that way of life, which was once so powerful and is now quickly vanishing. In the West everyone assumed that communism was a great evil. There were certainly aspects that were bad – evil even – but it wasn't all gray and dreary. There were bright things about it. For small children, it was a stimulating and welcoming place – a place where family came before anything else. It was also a place where humor was your best friend and resilience was your sister. The truth is, we were human beings just like everyone else. We had our dreams, our crushes, our petty animosities, and our great loves.

This is my story. It does not move in a straight line, but twists back over itself like a path through a Russian forest. So please bear with me. It's what life in the Soviet Union was like. It is what life everywhere is like.

And like life everywhere, it usually revolved around the kitchen.

OUT OF LINE

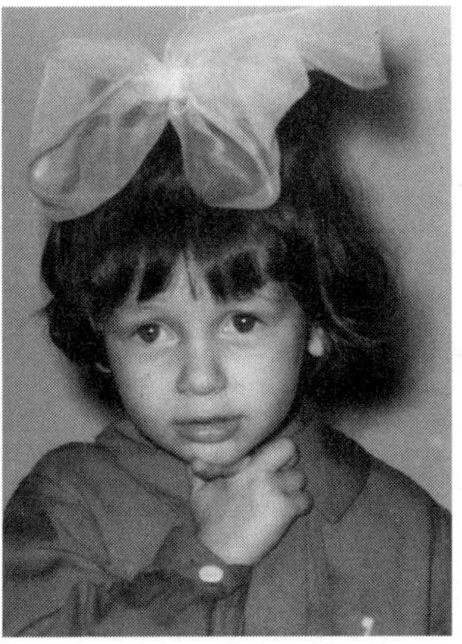

Baba Tina, the thoughtful observer
even at age four.

BABA TINA

IN OUR FAMILY, WE CALL 1972 A ROUND YEAR. THAT WAS THE YEAR THAT I TURNED TEN, MY PAPA TURNED FORTY, AND MY PATERNAL GRANDMOTHER, BABUSHKA INNA, TURNED SIXTY. SEPARATED BY several decades, we fit into each others' lives like a complete set of stacking Russian dolls, leaving no empty spaces inside.

Mama's dark hair was set in rollers in preparation for the big party that night. Her left hand on her hip, she commanded the gas stove like a symphony conductor who knew exactly what she could get out of her instruments. Something was simmering or boiling or warming on each of the four burners. Mama stirred the contents of one pot with a wooden spoon, tapped the spoon against its rim, blew on it, and sipped. She looked offended. "Tasteless!" she declared and threw a pinch of salt into the pot, and with a metal clang, banged the lid decisively into place. Then she moved on to another pot.

Stuffed cabbage in sweet-and-sour tomato sauce competed for pride of place with a skillet full of *katletkas*, ground chicken flavored with onions, garlic, and mushrooms, then fried carefully to golden perfection. In a pan on the front right burner were boiled potatoes that would be mixed with peas, pickles, shredded chicken, onions, eggs, and mayonnaise and turned into *alevye*, a salad that appears at every Russian celebration.

On the final burner, the one closest to the window, sat a large green pot full of compote. The steam made the windowpane weep and my heart rejoice. Prunes, dried apricots, pears, apples, and raisins bubbled together in a fragrant cinnamon-spiced stew.

I knew that eventually Mama would ask me to taste the dishes too. She would bring the wooden spoon to my lips and say, "Tell the truth. What is missing? Cinnamon? Sugar? Lemon juice?" Feeling important, I would close my eyes and render the verdict. It tasted heavenly.

"What's missing?"

I hesitated a moment. "Another potful!"

Everyone in the kitchen laughed and I did too. It was the morning of Papa's fortieth birthday dinner. I loved hearing other people's stories so much that I was called *Baba Tina* or nosy old woman. Standing in a kitchen full of gossip, good food, and my family, was my idea of paradise.

Mama's father, Dedushka Misha, was sitting in Mama's chair. Her mother, Babushka Bronya, sat in what was usually my papa's spot on a wooden stool at the small blue-and-white checkered table. Her back was propped against the side of our noisy refrigerator. She cut and sliced potatoes, cabbage, carrots, and onions.

Babushka's black dress with its creamy lace collar was protected by a spotless, frayed apron. Her swollen feet were tucked into Mama's worn-out slippers. Her fingers were stained with little brown flecks from years of cooking, cleaning, and harsh weather, but her face was white and smooth. Waves of gray hair were nestled in a pillowy braided bun on her neck. Babushka rarely smiled, but her features were serene. She looked lovely to me in the wintry morning light and I kissed her soft cheek. Even though she often hid her feelings behind her heavy, curtained eyelids, when she looked out on the world it was with a tender, sorrowful expression, as if someone had borrowed something of value from her and never returned it.

Babushka Bronya and Dedushka Misha had arrived to help Mama with the cooking and to use our shower before I was up. Their communal apartment had no hot water and no private shower, and it was February, a very cold month in Kiev. They were happy to help. Babushka Bronya thought Mama was the luckiest of women because she was married to my papa.

Both of my parents had grown up in the same communal apartment building following World War II. The Soviet Union had been through a four-year-long nightmare that swallowed young men, emptied whole neighborhoods, made millions of women widows, and left even more children fatherless. Among them were Babushka Inna, my father, and his younger brother, my Uncle Valentine.

Because Kiev had been occupied by the Nazis and had suffered more heavy damage when it was liberated by the Soviet army, few buildings remained standing. Under one roof, many families shared a kitchen, bathrooms, and showers. Under such circumstances, bitter enemies and fast friends were often made. My grandmothers chose to become friends.

Babushka Inna was the sole support of her two sons and her elderly parents. She worked hard and her days were long. As a result, Papa and Uncle Valya were often left to fend for themselves. Babushka Bronya and other neighbors kept a fond eye on them, but even so, they spent much of their time with other mischievous, hungry boys, whose fathers had not returned from the war.

Even though Inna's older son ran around the neighborhood with a pack of wild boys, Bronya was always fond of him. According to her, Papa was never really one of them. When Babushka Bronya found out that a group of boys had stolen a neighbor's chicken and had roasted and eaten it in the nearby cemetery, she refused to believe that my father was involved. Nevertheless, perhaps secretly hoping that a well-placed bribe might mean that the neighbor's hens would be left in peace, she lured Papa home with a plate of potato dumplings, and while he ate, she mended a suspicious tear in his trousers.

Skinny-legged, feisty, Mama had captured my tender papa's heart when they were children playing outside the dismal building. She was only twenty when, wearing a simple dress and

My parents on their wedding day.

holding a large bouquet of flowers, she married him. My sister, Natasha, and I spent our first years in the communal apartment.

To my romantic papa, Mama was the most beautiful woman in the world and he often told her so. I loved to see him find Mama at the stove, wrap his arms around her waist, and bury his nose in the nape of her neck. His love was returned. In the weeks leading up to his birthday, Mama froze standing in food lines, and carried heavy bags up three flights of stairs, all so that in every dish she would serve that night, you could taste her love for him.

Like most people who live together, my parents sometimes fought. Mama's outbursts were short-lived. Her pale skin turned pink, she used a colorful word or two, banged her lids against her pots, and then it was over. Papa's way of fighting was quieter, but more deadly. He simply put down his knife and fork and stopped eating Mama's cooking. He stewed, simmered, and steamed like the big green pot on Mama's stove. Not eating was a powerful weapon in a country where no happy husband is a thin husband. But in the end, they always found something to laugh about and the storm passed. Their only ongoing disagreement was over Papa's job.

Papa spoke and acted like a scholar even though, like other children of his generation, he had little formal education. His schooling had ended in eighth grade. Despite Papa's passion for books – his precious library lined the hallway in our apartment on bookshelves he built himself – he deliberately chose to work in a foundry, because in Soviet Ukraine a manual worker could make much more money than a doctor or a lawyer or an engineer.

It was hard work. He left at five in the morning to make his way to the steel plant. At times, as the steel was poured, it would splash, and despite Papa's heavy gear, it left deep, nasty burns on his legs. Mama begged him to find other less dangerous work, but he wouldn't hear of it. Providing his family with as much comfort as possible in a place where comforts were meager meant more to him than the grueling hours he spent in the hellish foundry.

Although Papa left his wild boyhood friends behind, the rebel in him was never completely quenched. It was Papa who named us. In our culture names are very significant. Your name not only tells the world about you, but also about the people who came before you, because your father's name, adjusted for gender, is added to yours. My older sister was given the classic Russian name, Natasha. But when Mama was pregnant with me, the actress and great beauty (but not as beautiful as Mama, Papa was quick to point out), Natalya Fatyeva, starred in a war movie called *Ambush on the Way*. Papa liked the independent, brave heroine of the film, and her name, Tina.

Tina was such an unusual name in Ukraine that at the birth registry, the Soviet official, a stocky woman with a tight bun, looked disapprovingly over her wire-rimmed glasses at Papa. He was holding me, a heavy blanket-bundle.

"Comrade Grimberg, are you sure you do not want to give your daughter a more common name so that she does not stand out?"

"No," said Papa, smiling. "I like this name."

"As you wish, but remember, I warned you!" she said curtly. She pounded the registration papers with her stamp, as if she were sentencing me to a lifetime of being out of step.

The kitchen was buzzing. Zina, one of our neighbors, came by to borrow flour and an egg. "Svetochka," she said, cupping the egg with one hand and her watermelon breast with the other. "My chest does not feel good inside. Something tells me I should be worrying about my husband."

Mama sighed at just the right moment, and rubbed her own chest in sympathy. "Zinochka, find me somebody who does feel good here." They simultaneously exhaled a heavy *Oy*. Satisfied at being so thoroughly understood, Zina said good-bye, and Fanya, another neighbor from across the hallway, took her place.

Like rising dough, Fanya's soft body filled in the remaining space between the table and the wooden cabinet my father built for our everyday china and glass jars of pickles, tomatoes, and mushrooms. Fanya didn't work and her children lived far away, so her life was a narrow one. She made up for it with boundless curiosity about other people's lives – ours in particular. On this day, Mama was grateful for her help. Because Fanya and her husband were kind to us, and because we would have had nothing to sit on in our apartment that night (Papa and Fanya crossed the tiny cement passage between our apartments many times, carrying furniture back and forth. Her dining room table and kitchen chairs were squeezed into our apartment to make space for eating and dancing, and much of our furniture migrated across to Fanya's for the night) and nothing to eat (our party food had taken over every inch in Fanya's refrigerator and tiny freezer), Mama invited them to the party.

Fanya and her husband, Gutnick, lived in an apartment identical to ours. Nobody ever called Gutnick by his first name, so Gutnick he remained to everyone. On long winter evenings Papa often announced "I will go see the Gutnicks" and stepped across the hallway for a cup of tea and a little conversation. I begged to go along. Papa lovingly called me his *chvostick* or little tail. Fanya offered me their box of chessmen and I happily sat on the sofa arranging the figures while, being careful not to be noticed, I watched in fascination as Gutnick awkwardly swung his clubfoot under the table.

Fanya is a relic, a leftover. She was born in a small Jewish settlement somewhere near Kiev. She married early, and she never worked outside her home. Because she remembered something of the old, pre-Revolutionary world, she was a storehouse of information about holidays and customs that were now forbidden, and in whispers she tried to pass what she knew on to us.

We shared a small conspiracy, Fanya and I. Every year when the leaves began to turn red, a day came when I found a gift on our kitchen table. A thin, white linen napkin covered a little china plate, its silver rim almost worn away. On it sat two pieces of honey cake. I knew it was Fanya who left the treat, but something told me not to ask her about it or thank her. I did know that honey cake symbolized a sweet new year, the arrival of the Jewish New Year, but I didn't want to know more. It would be many years before a whole honey cake was served from my table at Rosh Hashanah.

The only person missing from the kitchen on that cold morning was Natasha. Although I shared Mama and Papa's adoration of her, so much so that I imitated everything she did, including the ways she walked, chewed her food, and daintily pressed her napkin to her lips, I was thrilled to have all the grown-ups to myself for once. Natasha was curled up in the other room like an elegant cat, reading one of the classical Russian novels that Mama approved of.

Natasha, with her jet-black hair, dark eyes, and gorgeous legs was five and a half years older than I. We went to the same school and even shared some teachers, who often commented "You are a Grimberg, but you are not Natasha."

Mama did her best to dress Natasha beautifully, something that took Herculean effort. Simply going to a store to buy a dress or a pair of shoes was often fruitless. The shelves were either empty, or what they have held had been designed for collective farm women, not for the delicate Natasha. Mama had to rely on connections, or *proteczia*. She had to find someone who knew

The good student, Natasha, in our kitchen.

someone who had a pipeline to goods from overseas that would never make it onto store shelves. This precious merchandise was shared among store managers and salesclerks, and you had to know the right people, as well as be willing to pay extra rubles for the items. Sometimes Mama's entire salary was spent on Natasha's clothing, but Mama had grown up in a country ruined by war and, along with her family, she suffered the deprivations of poverty. Seeing Natasha so well dressed gave her great pleasure.

I loved beautiful things too, but my turn had not yet come, according to Mama and Papa. Until it did, I wore the clothes that Natasha had outgrown or that Mama made for me. I coped with little grace, throwing a loud fit when something pretty for Natasha arrived.

It's true that Natasha loved me, but mostly I annoyed her. Even so, despite her frustrations with me, she never let go of my hand when we crossed the street on our way to school. And woe to any boy who took up with me in class.

Natasha knew how I hated my big ears, and after she caught me eavesdropping on her as she gossiped with her friends about boys, she threw me out of our bedroom. "The reason your ears are so big is because you want to hear everything!" she said.

I had ways of taking revenge. Our voices were alike. When her boyfriend called and I answered the phone, I pretended to be her and tried to draw a declaration of love out of him. Eventually, he caught on, and my big ears were mentioned again.

The Baba in me hated to miss a thing. I wanted to stay in the kitchen taking everything in, but between the steaming pots, my grandmother's heavy sighs, and Fanya's generous hips, I was in the way. Mama decided that I was being idle, and being idle was not allowed.

"Do you have homework, Tina?"

"No."

Mama threw me a quick, penetrating glance. She knew I was not telling the whole truth. She began again.

"Tina," there was a tinge of ice in her voice and I felt panicky. When Mama got upset enough, she emptied my schoolbag and that was the last thing I wanted. She'd find leftovers from last week's lunches, some notes from my girlfriend, Irina, and a book or two. Not only had I not done my homework, but I couldn't even remember what I was supposed to do. It was hard to pay attention to assignments when I could hide a novel inside the covers of a textbook and read all the way through math class.

This time I was lucky. Sensing danger, Babushka Bronya came to my rescue. "Svetochka, leave her. We are about to celebrate."

But Mama was determined to make me useful. "Tinochka, get dressed and go outside to meet Babushka Inna. She'll need help with her packages. When you get back, you can change, because the guests will be here soon."

I was exiled from the warm kitchen, but because it was for my other grandmother, Papa's mama, I didn't grumble. It was bitterly cold outside. It took ages to get dressed for a Kiev February morning. Keeping warm outside, especially while waiting for endless hours in food lines or at bus stops, required effort and wit. My coat and hat were well lined, and I topped them with a heavy scarf and mittens. I wore heavy woolen socks and a pair of tights tucked into brown fur-lined boots. If I heard someone behind me calling my name, I would have to turn my entire body to reply. Dressed in my warm, black-trimmed, red sheepskin coat I closed the apartment door behind me and ventured out.

Downstairs, the walkway to the street was deserted. It was too cold even for the old women who usually gathered on the benches. I felt the fresh wintry air in my nostrils, wrapped my arms around one of the three chestnut trees that stood in front of our building, and swung myself around it, waiting for Babushka Inna. Looking up into the bare branches I could see the pale sky and a dusty morning sun.

I pretended that the chestnut trees were my three shining knights – tall, broad-shouldered, and long of arm. My father planted them the year we moved into the building. In the spring their leaves, wide as the palm of one's hand, supported tiny candelabra-like flowers. They pointed toward the sky, rising above our oppressive daily lives. Their roots ran deep and protruded through the asphalt pavement of the walkway like veins on the hand of an old woman.

Hearts were scratched into the trunks, along with lovers' names that lasted long after the lovers themselves had forgotten each other. I traced these hearts with my fingers and learned that Kolya loved Oksana. To prove it, Kolya's heart was pierced with an arrow. But further down, a knife had cut cruelly into the trunk, declaring that Kolya now loved Lusu. I saw Kolya's name on one of the other trees. I decided that Kolya was truly a romantic, tormented soul, who more than anything or anyone in the world, loved to torture trees.

Finally, I could see my grandmother Inna's figure at the end of the street. I forgot trying to mimic Natasha's elegant walk and ran as fast as I can, stiff-legged and muffled in my winter clothes. She dropped her packages to the frozen ground, laughed, and scooped me up in a perfumed, exuberant hug. Against the fresh morning snow, in her black winter coat trimmed with fur collar, with her bravely painted lips, she looked like a *czarina*, a queen, to me.

Whereas Babushka Bronya was everything comfortable and homey, Babushka Inna was fascinating and exotic. She always had patient answers to my many questions and was full of stories about Papa when he was a little boy and about Dedushka David, who had died before I was born. All her stories were punctuated with liquor-filled chocolates, or better yet, a small bite of caviar spread over white bread with butter. She did not talk about her time in prison.

Babushka Inna, Papa's mama.

Joseph Stalin was the leader of the Soviet Union from 1929 to 1953. After World War II and the defeat of Nazi Germany, the peace that followed was an uneasy one. Stalin was a cruel and ruthless dictator. His secret police were everywhere, watching ordinary citizens with what seemed like X-ray vision. For the slightest reason, real or imagined, people could be sent to prison. All it took was a charge of disloyalty to the state. Careless gossip, offended neighbors, or petty jealousies were very dangerous during these years. They were called the Yezhov Terror, and they were named after Nikolai Yezhov, the Chief of Police, who carried out Stalin's dirty work. Eventually even Stalin turned against him and had him executed, but not before millions and millions of people had died in the gulags or Siberian labor camps. Everyone came to dread the late-night knock at the door. The Terror could visit anyone.

It visited Babushka Inna when my father was only twelve years old, leaving him alone to stand for months outside a forbidding, windowless brick building, waiting for word, any word of his mother.

The night two men and a woman came to arrest Inna, her frightened neighbors scurried into their own apartments like mice when a cat is near. Her sons were terrified and bewildered. Inna was terrified too, but she was not bewildered. The trouble had started months ago across the street from their apartment where a white brick factory stood. Several hundred men and women worked there, canning fish, meat, and vegetables. Inna was among them. She was organized and good at math, and soon she was running her department with skill and energy.

Everyone wanted to work in the canning factory. In a poverty-stricken country where food supplies were short and unpredictable, working near food was a very good thing. It meant that your family did not go hungry – as long as you didn't mind being a thief. Everyone understood that to steal something from your friend or neighbor was wrong, but stealing from the state was far more excusable. It was a matter of survival.

One of the doors of Inna's department opened into another building that housed a social club. The door sported a rusty lock that could have been broken by a pair of determined bare hands. The club was run by a notorious lady's man, Comrade Zupkov.

For months, Comrade Zupkov had stood at a dirt-streaked upstairs window and watched my grandmother cross the street to the canning plant. Her shapely figure, white skin, and long, dark hair were appealing, but not as appealing as her job. If only she was willing to cooperate, the door between her department and the social club could be the way to riches for both of them. If she would help Zupkov steal food, he could sell it on the black market.

Zupkov went to work on Inna. Compliments, flowers, and perfume followed, one after the other. Even though he was smooth and she was a lonely widow with two young boys, my grandmother was not interested.

When charm didn't work, Comrade Zupkov tried another tack. He asked Inna to become his business partner. If she would only help Zupkov smuggle supplies from her department into the social club, he would give her a cut of the profits. Inna said no.

"I am a mother and an honest woman, Zupkov. What will you tell your children if the police should come for you? The authorities *will* come for you one fine, bright day. Don't come near me again."

Zupkov was furious. "I assume this will stay between us, Inna Aronovna," he said stiffly.

At the plant, Inna ordered her staff to place a number of heavy boxes against the door between the factory and the social club, and she kept Zupkov's proposition to herself.

One fine, bright day, the Soviet police did come, but not for

Zupkov. It was Inna who was charged with stealing food from the factory. Because of an allegation against her, the police had done a quick stock-taking in her department and saw that inventory was missing. Stunned and shaken, without an opportunity for good-byes from her children, Babushka Inna was taken to the women's prison to await trial.

Inna was put into a cell with twenty or thirty other women. Some of them were angry and dangerous. Others were there because they had fought back against abusive husbands. Some were political prisoners, and there were others, like Inna, who were wrongly accused. Wide-eyed and wounded, the shock of arrest was still obvious on their faces, months after the police had come for them.

The matron in charge of Inna's cell, rough and crudely spoken, grew to like my grandmother. She was the one to suggest ways for Inna to survive. She herself kept a keen eye on troublemakers, and she advised Inna to give some of her food to the toughest of them. Inna shared what little she had and that helped to appease and hold the most dangerous prisoners at bay.

But it was Inna's unusual education that helped her weather the ordeal. She relied on it to escape, at least in her imagination, from the dirt of the cell and the smell of the toilets and cold showers.

Inna was a young girl after the Communist Revolution in 1917. She and her parents were allocated two small rooms in a mansion that had once belonged to a nobleman.

The nobleman had had the opportunity to escape to France, but had stayed in Kiev because his son was fighting in the White Army for the czar. Captured by Soviet officers, the young man was led to the nearby forest and shot. After his son was killed, the nobleman became a recluse and for nearly two years refused to leave his room. His daughters were as devastated as he was. They never thought of leaving each other or their father to marry. Instead, they poured all their attention on the young, dark-eyed, bright Inna.

They had been educated by French governesses and private tutors. Now, confined to a room or two in the house that had been their estate, they made Inna their student. They taught her everything they knew: languages, literature, geography, and history. They put on plays and charades as entertainments. Through these women, aristocratic and smelling of jasmine, Inna had learned to love what was beautiful. The two sisters had given her a priceless gift that her loving parents, who grew up in a *shtetl*, a small Jewish town, could not – a fine liberal arts education.

In prison, Inna was able to put that education to unexpected use. In the crowded cell she helped the women who possessed little education to read court documents, and she acted as a scribe for the ones who wrote poorly. She told stories from the books she'd read, and recounted the history of great Russian heroes to help pass the tedious hours. Even the hardest of the prisoners loved a good story. Inna's cellmates grew to respect her, and they left her in peace.

After Inna had been in prison for several months, the police raided her apartment on Stretskaya Street to search for the money from the stolen goods that they thought she must have hidden. The hallways of the apartment building, usually so noisy and busy, fell silent.

The men were stunned by what they found. Inna's elderly parents and her young sons, Papa and Uncle Valya, lived in one room. The room had no dresser or sideboard for storage. A friend had made them a cardboard trunk, and in it they stored clothes and bedding. As a boy, my father often slept in the trunk to escape from cockroaches and mosquitoes. Four iron beds were lined up against whitewashed walls. In the middle of the room stood a small wooden table surrounded by four chairs. That was all.

The men pawed through the family's meager belongings. They found nothing. Eyes cast down, they closed the door quietly behind them when they left.

Their grandparents tried to take care of Papa and Uncle Valya, but the two boys, unruly and restless, paid little attention to them. What small salary the old people had was spent to pay for Babushka Inna's food in jail.

When Inna was taken away, my great-grandmother became a prisoner too, isolated by deafness and depression. As the months dragged on and there was little hope of freeing Inna, her health declined and her depression deepened. She died without seeing her daughter freed or her name cleared. Inna was not allowed to attend her mother's funeral.

The neighbors helped. They understood that Stalin's police could knock on anyone's door. Everyone lived in a kind of twilight of fear and suspicion. They ached for those unjustly accused, but they had to remain silent. Any one of them could have suffered

Joseph Stalin; eyes that saw everything.

Inna's fate, and they knew it. All they could do was to treat Papa and Uncle Valya with kindness while Inna was away.

Babushka Bronya often fed Papa, but the arrest meant the end of his education. Since his mother's salary was lost, Papa had to quit school and go to work. Perhaps because they felt some kind of obligation, the people at the canning factory overlooked his age and hired him.

For eleven months, every Wednesday, Papa left home at four in the morning with a bundle of food to take his place in the long line outside the jail. At some point the gates would open, and family members would flood into the prison courtyard. Direct contact between family and inmates was forbidden, but if the guards were in a good mood, they passed along the heavy bags of food from the visitors.

Papa's uncles did what they could for their sister-in-law. They hired an attorney and managed to send a bit of money to their nephews. It wasn't enough to feed the hungry teenagers. Papa developed a liking for pigeon during those long months. He hunted the birds with a slingshot and roasted them in the cemetery woods near where the chicken had suffered its fate a few years earlier.

Valya was more creative. Around Easter, Ukrainian Orthodox Christians would visit the graves of their loved ones with a meal that they would eat in the cemetery. To augment his diet, Valya would proclaim "Christ has risen!" In return he often received a brightly painted egg.

The missing inventory was found eventually. The cans of food were in the boxes that had been piled up to block the door to the social club. The person who had denounced Inna to the authorities was none other than Comrade Zupkov.

As Inna's trial date neared, Zupkov retired from the social

club, but his flowers and gifts of perfume eventually worked on another lonely widow. Not for long, though. During one passionate night he died in her lonely embrace.

Inna was proclaimed innocent and was released. Papa borrowed money from his uncles and bought a cake. The family wept. Inna walked out of the courthouse whispering, "Hot bath is what I want. Hot bath!"

Many years have passed and I have heard fragments of the story from others, never from Inna herself. Babushka Inna no longer lived on Stretskaya Street. She had a small room in the heart of Kiev and spent over an hour on the bus in order to see us. Since the center of Kiev housed universities, government buildings, theaters, and museums, she brought with her a glamorous, cosmopolitan air. What's more, she had connections.

In a place where food was scarce, her job was the envy of many. She trained people who worked in grocery stores around the city. She took me shopping with her once, and it was an adventure. We walked into a store and took our place at the end of a long line. In no time, one of the clerks, a student of Inna's spotted us. She smiled, flashing three gold teeth, and motioned to us to step through a side door. Holding Inna's hand, I followed her into a dark corridor full of wet cartons, brooms, and smelly mops. The gold-toothed lady handed my grandmother a newspaper package. "Inna Aronovna, it came this morning so it is fresh. Enjoy!"

I was amazed. With no private sector or competition, customer service was non-existent. I had never met a clerk who smiled at a customer in a store, much less in a dark corridor. But Soviet life was all about who you knew. Jobs like these gave little people a lot of power, and they used it.

Out on the street, I asked what was in the package.

"Take a look."

I folded back a corner of newspaper. It was a beautifully smoked fish, and beside it, Papa's favorite, a hard red salami.

By the time Babushka Inna and I got upstairs, Fanya had gone home to get ready for the party. The two grandmothers began their greeting ritual. It consisted of an elaborate exchange of numbers: their blood pressures, heart rates, addresses of newly discovered doctors, dosages of newly prescribed pills. At times they even shared the medicines they carried in their purses.

Mama unwrapped Inna's packages. Red paltus, smoked fish, hard burgundy salami, chocolates, and even mandarin oranges. "Thank you, Inna Aronovna. These things will be wonderful on the table!"

Even though Mama had known Inna since she was a little girl, she called her by the formal name, but the two women had more in common than they would admit. For one thing, they both loved Papa, Natasha, and me. They both were spirited and opinionated, and their inevitable clashes were usually followed by a period of cold "peace" that I hated. Eventually, there was always reconciliation, and the smoked fish and salami appeared on our table again.

There was one other thing they had in common. Both Mama and Babushka Inna had shed their Jewish-sounding birth names. Mama was born *Sarah*. When she was a small girl, children teased her, calling her *Sarochka, Sarochka, Jidovchka*, or little kike. She went home and stated firmly that from then on she would answer only to the name *Svetlana*. Similarly, Babushka Inna had changed her name from the Jewish *Ginda* when she began to go to school. Years passed before these names were used again. Sarah would become part of my Hebrew name, and Inna would one day call herself Ginda again.

Natasha and I spread a white, starched tablecloth over the mismatched tables that had been pushed together to accommodate everybody. A rule Mama shared with all other Russians: Nobody ate standing in our home. Civilized people sat and talked and drank, facing one another. The seats had various pedigrees, from carved dining-room chairs to plastic stools. Even the sofa had been pushed up to the table, and pillows were piled to make up for the differences in height.

We set the table with our holiday dishes, white with navy rims, and crystal salad bowls and platters. As if we were butlers wearing starched shirts and heavy appliquéd coats from an old Russian novel, Natasha and I carried platters to the table with arms outstretched and backs straight. We made a sharp turn back to the kitchen and checked ourselves in the mirror every time we passed. Next to sampling the food, this was my favorite thing – arranging the platters to make the table look beautiful. We laid out a mosaic of chopped liver, herring salad, pickled cucumbers, tomatoes, mushrooms, salad alevye, gefilte fish in jellied broth, devilled eggs, and more. And that was for starters.

The guests began to arrive and I was kissed, hugged, and judged to be too skinny. Despite it being the bleak and frigid beginning of February, people had brought flowers, as well as wine and vodka, all wrapped in *Pravda* (the newspaper whose name meant *truth*), and stored on the balcony to keep them cold. *Pravda* was the national joke that everybody knew, but nobody dared to repeat in public. Every time someone used it for wrapping herring or pickles, lining a cat's litter box, or as a desperate substitute for toilet paper, the thought was always there – *it's good for something, but not for the truth.*

When the apartment was full of friends and family, everybody sported the imprint of someone's lipstick kiss on their cheek. We filled our plates with food, but no one would think of starting before the first toast was given. My uncle Valya, Papa's brother, acted as the *tamada*, the one responsible for the flow of the entertainment. Valya led us in toasts to Papa and then to Babushka Inna, who sat proudly between her sons. Then there were toasts to Mama, to children, to health, and to friends. Each toast was followed by a shot of ice-cold vodka for the men and wine for the rest of us.

Mama was praised again and again for raising such polite, charming daughters. I blushed and smiled, for it was rare that we were complimented to our faces. Adults seemed to think that praise would go to young people's heads and they would stop working to improve themselves.

Eventually, the time came when my cousins and I were expected to go into the other room because the next part of the evening was for the grown-ups. The talk would turn to sex and politics, not suitable subjects for children. In the past, my cousins and I had tried to sneak back into the room and hide under the table, but our giggles had always given us away. Now I was older and I tried another tactic: I started clearing the dishes from the first course. It worked, and I was pleased. Now I'd be able to hear Uncle Valya tell his favorite stories.

Faina Ranevskaya

Uncle Valya was an amateur actor and director who spent many of his evenings and weekends involved with theater for young people. He told stories about the theater with his entire being. His eyebrows moved. His eyes flashed. His cheeks and chin were involved. I loved to hear him talk about Faina Ranevskaya, a legendary actress with a quick wit. Once, a melodramatic cast member of a play exclaimed, "You want my death! I can sense it. And you will be happy to come to my funeral and spit on my grave." Ranevskaya responded, "I hate standing in line!"

The roomful of people, all of them knowing far too much about standing in lines, roared.

Uncle Valya was not finished. "After one of her performances, Ranevskaya was standing in her dressing room, totally naked, smoking her cigarette. The director of the theater walked in unannounced and froze. Without missing a beat, Ranevskaya said, 'Are you shocked that I smoke?'" The laughter bubbled up again and glasses were refilled.

When the bottles of vodka and wine were nearly empty and the toasts expanded to include neighbors, colleagues, and people of goodwill in general, it was time for the dancing to start. Someone turned on the record player. Part of the fun was dancing with someone other than your spouse. Papa danced with a friend of Mama's. Mama danced with Valya.

Records were censored by the Soviet authorities, so each LP included songs filled with Soviet propaganda. We didn't care. As long as "The Glory of Lenin" and "Our Party's Dream, Communism, Is in Sight" had a good beat, we danced anyway.

The evening ended with a cousin sitting down to play Yiddish melodies on the piano. I was familiar with the tunes and they moved me, but I was not sure why. Only the adults remembered the words and they sang along. Then it was time for final kisses and good-byes. Mama was satisfied, but exhausted. Natasha and I cleared the dishes and stood on the balcony to shake the tablecloth full of crumbs in the cold, fresh air. We turned back and saw Mama, standing in front of the mirror in the kitchen, taking the pins out of her hair. Papa was kissing both her arms, gently, gently.

Little Tina, in holiday dress at Childcare #47.
Big Lenin is in the background, as he always was.

Little Lenin

LITTLE LENIN

SINCE ALMOST ALL SOVIET WOMEN WORKED, RELIABLE, INEXPENSIVE CHILDCARE WAS ESSENTIAL. WE WERE DROPPED OFF IN THE MORNINGS AT CHILDCARE CENTERS WHERE WE PLAYED, SANG, DANCED, drew, and sculpted all day. In the evenings we'd play outside, watched by caretakers, until our parents or grandparents picked us up. Much was miserable about Soviet life, as I would learn, but not the stimulating, well organized care we got as small children.

A life-sized statue of a young Lenin greeted everyone who walked through the worn wooden doors into the lobby of Childcare Center #47. Made of white alabaster, Lenin was depicted as a little boy, no more than eight years old. He wore carved, short pants that ended at his knees and his neat, belted shirt was primly buttoned up to his chin. A book was tucked under his arm. His thoughtful gaze was directed into the distance, suggesting, even promising, a better future for the tired and unjustly treated masses of Russian people. I had a crush on him.

In the Soviet Union, statues, paintings, and photos of Lenin were everywhere you looked: in the squares, on billboards, and at street corners. They were meant to remind citizens of their good fortune in living the Soviet way of life. The creator of all that good fortune was Vladimir Ilyich Lenin, the father of the Soviet Revolution. He was born to an educated, middle-class family in 1870, at a time when there was a yawning gap between social classes, terrible working conditions for the poor, and widespread child labor. Inspired by Karl Marx, Lenin championed education for all, free medical care, an eight-hour working day, and group (or collective) farms where harvests and livestock would be owned collectively by the people, and profits would be shared equally among them.

For Russia, the turn of the 20th century brought chaos: World War I, famine, and social unrest rocked the country. Factories and plants often went on strike and the ruling monarch, the czar and his White Army, used brutal violence to restore order. It is easy to understand why Lenin's rebellious ideas were so appealing.

On several occasions activists had tried to assassinate the czar. They weren't successful and eventually they were captured and hanged. One of them was Lenin's older brother. Lenin wanted more than a dead czar who would be replaced by yet another czar, who might or might not make life better for most people. He believed that what Russia needed was a complete change in the order of things. Revolution seemed to be the only answer.

Headed by Lenin, the October Revolution of 1917 turned the country upside down. Civil war followed, the czar and his family were assassinated, and in the end, victory was claimed by the revolutionary Red Army. Socialism was established as a stepping stone toward communism. In the not-too-distant future, the Soviet nation was to evolve into a communist society where everything was shared and where each individual would work for the benefit of others. Within a few years, there was no more illiteracy. Children no longer had to sleep on factory floors. There was an opportunity for education. There was free medical care and university education. There was no more homelessness.

From birth we were taught about Lenin and what he stood for. In Soviet society, the truth and value of his ideas were not to be questioned.

Most statues of Lenin were huge and imposing. He would be shown standing confidently, holding his worker's cap in one hand, as if he were about to speak to a mob of avid listeners. His outstretched arm and his bare head served as inviting perches for migrating birds and pigeons. Around the entire city, official ceremonies of all kinds took place in the shadow of Lenin's various firmly planted bronze feet. These were usually accompanied by orchestras enthusiastically playing Red Army marches. I happily moved up through the ranks of Lenin's youth groups on my way to becoming a full-fledged communist, first as a little *Oktyabryonok*, and later as a teen Pioneer with a red kerchief to wear around my neck, all at the base of one of his statues.

Long before I understood the Soviet Union's stormy and complicated history, I was crazy about the statue of Little Lenin that stood in the lobby of Childcare Center #47. He looked like a boy I'd want to have as a friend. Although he was placed on a pedestal, he was like any of the other small children at Childcare #47, only better. We were taught that we should be like Lenin was when he was a little boy: honest, hardworking, and polite. He was, in every way, a model child.

Mama was a teacher at #47, and she had been bringing me to work with her since I was a baby. I had grown up thinking of Little Lenin as my personal friend. Though I was now ten and had long since moved on to regular school, I often went back to catch up with my old teachers and caregivers. During one of those visits, I learned that the lobby of Childcare Center #47 was about to be renovated. The statue of Little Lenin, which had grown shabby from years of sticky-handed preschoolers' affectionate handling, would have no place in the new lobby. The thought of Lenin not greeting small children distressed me. What a waste! It was terrible to dispose of someone who led a blameless life, never lying, never being rude, and always finishing his homework on time. All he needed was a gentle bath, a lick of white plaster to fill in the chips, and Little Lenin would be as good as new.

A plan, delicious and tempting, took root in my mind and obstinately refused to leave it. What if I could rescue Little Lenin and bring him to my new school? He could stand in our homeroom. No other class had such a thing. I could only imagine the surprise and envy of my classmates when they learned that I was the one who was responsible for the presence of Little Lenin in our midst. The thought made me light-headed. On the first day of the upcoming school year, after the opening ceremony, our teacher, Nina Petrovna, would lead our class of forty or so to the second floor, pause dramatically, and with both arms she'd push open the double doors. Silent awe would give way to gasps of delight at the sight of Little Lenin. When my classmates could finally tear their respectful eyes from the statue, their gaze would turn to me. Modestly, I would look away.

Mama agreed that saving Little Lenin was a wonderful idea, and everyone at Childcare Center #47 thought it would be good for Little Lenin to have a new home. The statue was carefully washed, the chips were touched up with plaster, and it was swaddled in the folds of soft old blankets. Papa and I watched as a mover – cigarette hanging from the corner of his mouth, dirty white undershirt revealing an abundant carpet of dark chest hair – circled a heavy rope around Lenin's body as if, given a chance, the stone child might run away.

The man lifted Little Lenin into the air and stowed him on a bed of straw in the back of a small truck. Then he gathered up the hammer and assorted greasy wrenches that littered the back seat to make room for Papa and me.

Feeling pleased with myself, I looked at Papa as we made a sharp turn out of Childcare Center #47 and set off for the school. The dust rose from the bumpy road and mixed with the smell of sweat and liquor coming from the front seat. Papa smiled back at me.

Nina Petrovna met us outside the empty school building and led the way upstairs to the door of our homeroom. The mover, Little Lenin in his arms, grunted as he followed her while Papa and I brought up the rear, our footsteps echoing in the corridor that would bustle with students and teachers once school began. When Nina Petrovna unlocked the door and pointed to a table, I could see the faint trace of a smile on her dour face.

It was strange to be in my classroom before school had started. Some things were different. Through the big window that looked out onto a small green hill and a cement pathway, I could see that the fruit trees, tended by our science teacher and the students last spring, had grown over the summer. Now they stood tall on sturdy whitewashed trunks. Some things were the same. Opposite the window, the door of the broom closet still hung from one hinge, and I could see the mops, buckets, and sponges that were stored in it. At the end of the school day, pairs of us would take turns staying late to sweep, mop, and dust the classrooms. We hated the chores, but not as much as we hated the thought of a visit to the school principal for shirking our communal duty.

Little Lenin was placed on a red draped table, looking as proud and thoughtful as ever.

My class would be the envy of the whole school. All the other students had to rely on photographs of Lenin to inspire them. We had an actual statue.

When Nina Petrovna thanked the mover with a curt nod, I could see the dark roots of her blonde head. As she locked the door to the classroom, she turned to me, her thin, pale lips straining up at the corners. "Fine job, Grimberg. Our leader will serve as a good example to the pupils! I will see you in a few days."

I skipped all the way home at Papa's side.

The last days of summer were spent getting ready for the school year. All around the neighborhood, in fact all around the country, clotheslines had sprouted school uniforms. Mama washed my brown wool tunic and apron in cold water and hung them out on the balcony to dry. Late that night, when the uniform had finally dried, Mama sewed a white lace collar over the brown one and pressed it with a warm iron. Crisp and fresh, the uniform was draped neatly over the chair in our bedroom, alongside a pair of pure white stockings and a new leather book bag.

The next day, the first of September, I set off for school looking neat and clean with the customary bouquet of flowers for the teacher in my arms. I joined hundreds of other girls and boys as we gathered in the schoolyard to hear the principal's address and other speeches. The principal, in her black suit, high-heeled sandals, and liberally applied red lipstick, stood at the wooden podium. A red banner that read "*Uchitsa, uchitsa, uchitsa*, Study, study, study," flapped above her head. These were words that Lenin had spoken, and they appeared in every school building, library, and university.

Me at about age eight.

The principal called on us to make our homeland proud by getting good grades and by doing honest, hard work. She pursed her red lips. "The example set for us by our leaders, Lenin in particular, is a flame to guide us in achieving a communist future, a future that is just around the corner if we study and work hard!"

I beamed with happy anticipation. At last the ceremony ended. Just the way I'd imagined it, Nina Petrovna gathered all of us around her and asked us to form rows of twos as we waited our turn to enter the building. The other teachers looked tanned and rested after their summer, but Nina Petrovna seemed pale and a little sad. Even though her arms were filled with the bright asters and mums we'd brought her, her eyes were sorrowful.

Last year we'd been thrilled to watch romance budding between Nina Petrovna and the science teacher. She had appeared, one day, with her light brown hair dyed blonde, her dusty flat shoes exchanged for pointy black patent heels, and a bit of rouge standing out against her sallow cheeks. Later, there were exciting times when her admirer left love offerings – African violets or a mini cactus – on her desk. Everyone, even the boys, noticed that Nina Petrovna had become much kinder. Sometimes she even laughed.

Then came the morning when she took us to see the exotic tropical plants that the science teacher had received for the school's small greenhouse. The heat in the greenhouse reminded me of a *banya*, a Russian steam bath. Perspiring, we took off our coats and held them in our arms. We shifted from foot to foot on a narrow wet wooden path between the raised planters. When the science teacher passed by Nina Petrovna, he took advantage of the narrow walkway to brush against her back and pause there for a tiny second longer than necessary. My friend Zoyka and I nudged each other. Nina Petrovna blushed, straightened her back, and tightened the grip on her clipboard. Zoyka and I did not dare to look at each other because we knew we'd burst out laughing.

Later, in the snowy schoolyard, our coats draped over our shoulders, we did laugh as we reenacted the scene we'd just witnessed. After that there were many hurried conversations in the bathrooms about Nina Petrovna's upcoming wedding and maybe even a honeymoon.

At recess we often gathered in the school's auditorium to hear a girl named Galina play the piano. The teachers repaired to the staff room to smoke and drink tea, so we found it puzzling that the science teacher wanted to spend recess with a group of students, but we assumed that he was a music lover. Galina was older than I, and she could play any song or melody by ear. The science teacher would encourage her. "Galochka, Galochka, play another song for us!" Tall and slender, with long brown braids that almost brushed the keyboard, Galina swayed as she ran her fingers over the worn keys. We sang and clapped along with her. Closing her eyes and tilting her head, she could draw magic from that tired clunker of a piano.

One day when we got to the auditorium we found it locked. There was no music coming from within, and there was no sign of Galina. Instead, there were whispers that Galina had been sent home when the principal found her, pale and disoriented, outside the greenhouse in the dead of winter without her coat.

Not long after, the science teacher passed by our open classroom door with a stack of papers in his arms. His shoulders were stooped and he looked more like a hunted animal than a romantic hero. He barely glanced through our open door to where Nina Petrovna sat at her desk, grading papers. He adjusted his eyeglasses which were taped at the corner. We later learned that he'd picked up his battered black briefcase from the teachers' room and left the building, never to be seen again.

Rumors circulated around the school. Some people thought he just got tired of teaching. Others speculated that he must have returned to his family in southern Ukraine. But there were other, more disturbing rumors. Whatever the reason, when he disappeared, so did the air of romance that had lightened the halls of the school.

The African violets and mini cacti vanished from Nina Petrovna's desk, and soon so did Nina Petrovna, who left before the end of the school year to visit her ailing mother in a village outside Kiev.

When everyone returned from summer holidays, Nina Petrovna was the way she'd been before the science teacher had cast his eye her way, only she looked mousier than ever. All that was left of her lost love were the blonde tips of her hair.

We chattered loudly as we followed Nina Petrovna up the stairs to the second floor. Sashka was tugging the thick braid of his eternal love, Susanna, and Nikolai was throwing friendly punches at Igor. In short, everything was normal. We made our way down the long corridor, passing other rooms full of students already at their desks. We waved to people we knew. The usual class clowns made the usual faces and mildly obscene gestures to friends and foes alike. The only door that was still closed was ours.

Nina Petrovna drew us around her in the hallway and cleared her throat. "This year, our classroom has been graced with the presence of a very special guest, a guest you all love and cherish, a guest who will encourage you to learn and become better citizens of your homeland. Please behave accordingly and with the utmost respect!" My stomach lurched with the thrill of bringing the light of Little Lenin to my schoolmates.

Nina Petrovna finally opened the door and the students jostled to get inside.

I wasn't the first to enter, but it was soon clear to me that something had gone terribly wrong. Instead of awed, respectful silence, I heard someone laugh, quietly at first, and then with great horsey snorts of mirth. My heart sank.

Little Lenin was standing where Papa and I and Nina Petrovna had left him, but nobody could see his noble features or follow his thoughtful gaze into the future. His face was hidden under the metal waste can that somebody had upturned over his head. In addition to the book under his arm, he held a broom covered in dust balls.

Nina Petrovna rushed to Little Lenin and liberated him from the bin and broom. Using the dust rag, volunteers, gulping back their giggles, wiped away traces of his disgrace. I was afraid to look at the teacher. To my great relief she said nothing to me, or about me to the others. And she didn't say anything to the principal, either. Nina Petrovna threatened to take the matter into her unforgiving hands for further investigation, but all she did was pace between the rows of desks, making an awkward speech about shame and the disrespect shown to our great leader.

All that day I felt as if Lenin had turned his reproachful eyes from the glorious future to me. We never found out who desecrated the statue. It has remained a mystery to me and to Nina Petrovna to this day.

My grandparents and Mama in younger days.

MISHA AND BRONYA

EVERY DAY BABUSHKA BRONYA MADE THE LONG TREK BY BUS ACROSS KIEV TO LOOK AFTER ME, NATASHA, AND PAPA. "ONE SHOULD NOT ENTER AN EMPTY HOME," MAMA WOULD SAY, SO Babushka was always there to greet us at the door, wearing Mama's faded apron and slippers.

She had made sure the apartment was ready for when Papa got home, exhausted from the foundry, so that he could stretch out his legs on the plastic-covered yellow sofa, read the paper, have a cigarette, and try to nap. She placed his clean ashtray just so beside the sofa, prepared him a glass of tea, and tried to move about the small apartment as unobtrusively as possible. Papa was polite to Babushka, but they spoke little. I, on the other hand, talked and sang to her from the moment I got home.

I watched Babushka Bronya's fingers intently, as she peeled the flesh from the spine of a small herring and arranged the gray-pink nuggets around the rim of my plate so that they would look like flower petals and tempt me to eat. The center of the flower was a mound of mashed potatoes, heavy with milk and butter to make them as fattening as possible. Babushka (and everyone else) was concerned that I was too small for my age.

Even though I was nearly eleven and was certainly old enough to manage a piece of herring with bones by myself, I loved her for helping me. Her heavy-lidded eyes lowered and she hummed a nameless tune as she concentrated on the fish. If any bones were left, they were fine ones, no more dangerous than the few stubborn hairs on Babushka's chin.

I tried to make myself eat because I knew that, once I had finished my dinner and Babushka Bronya had visited with Mama, I was going to go with my grandmother back to Stretskaya Street to spend the night with her and Dedushka Misha. Tomorrow morning we were going to visit my aunt and cousin, Marina, on the other side of the Dnieper River. I lowered my head and inhaled the sweet, familiar smell of the potatoes on my plate. Mama was proud of our potatoes. Having potatoes that were free of mold all winter required planning and effort, and none of us took them for granted.

Because we were privileged to own a car, every fall Mama and Papa drove to the Beloruss countryside to buy food for the long, hard winter. They returned with a trunk full of mushrooms and firm, white potatoes. The mushrooms got marinated and took pride of place in the small cold cellar that Papa and a handful of trusted friends had dug between the bushes outside our apartment building. Papa had not asked for official permission because it was unlikely that permission would be granted.

It was worth the risk. There was no place to store food in our miniature kitchen so the cold cellar had enormous value.

Papa lined the cool opening in the earth with wooden shelves and placed a heavy iron gate over it. The neighbors muttered complaints to each other at first, but eventually they left us alone. As a result, we had healthy potatoes that tasted good throughout the endless winter.

Babushka was patient with me as I picked determinedly at my food and hummed a song I'd heard on the radio. Between refrains she asked about my day, my friends, and reminded me with a gentle nod to take another spoon of snowy mashed potatoes and their herring crown.

When Mama got home, had settled the daily cigarette conflict with Papa, and had taken up her command station at the stove, she and Babushka caught up on the day's news. As always, the Russian they spoke gave way to Yiddish. I knew they did this to keep certain things hidden from Natasha and me, but even though I was curious, I had no interest in learning Yiddish.

I finally finished eating enough to satisfy everyone and it was time to pack my things for the ride to Stretskaya Street. Against Babushka's protests, Mama filled a bag with butter, flour, and yeast for her to take home. She checked my knapsack to make sure I had everything I'd need, and Babushka and I set off together for the bus stop.

I tried to match my pace to her slow one, but it was difficult. I wanted so much to run. I loved to visit the little apartment on Stretskaya Street and the garden Dedushka Misha had scratched out on the patch of earth outside the crumbling apartment building. It was spring, and by now his lilac bushes and peonies would be in full bloom. If hooligans hadn't already ripped out the flowers for their red-cheeked girlfriends, I would be able to pick some and make a bouquet to take to my cousins in the morning.

It wasn't just Dedushka Misha's garden that I wanted to see. I was proud of my handsome grandfather, with his fine features and angular jaw. It was uncommon for a girl of my age to have a grandpa, much less a handsome one. Before they were even born, most of my friends had lost their grandfathers in the war with the Nazis. The few other grandfathers I knew had no hair except for small patches of it on the backs of their heads. Their pot bellies hung over pants held up by a set of braces.

My Dedushka had snow-white hair that was slightly yellow at the tips. He began every day with stretches and exercises, so his body was lean and flexible. I liked to watch him standing on one leg like a bird that had landed for a moment and was about to fly away again. Dedushka wanted to fly away all his life. Even though he had been born not far from Kiev, he felt like a stranger there.

He had studied agriculture at university, but the only outlet for his love of the earth and nature was the tiny scrap of garden and his lilacs, roses, and peonies. He longed for land of his own. The Soviet authorities frowned on people owning land, so Dedushka lived each day profoundly dissatisfied, storing his anger inside. Like a plant that cannot take root in a stony garden, Dedushka could not, would not, take root in Soviet soil.

He was utterly disillusioned by Soviet life. Soviet propaganda spoke of high ethics, but reality was a different matter. Despite all the slogans, people joked "They pretend they are paying us, and we pretend that we are working." Corruption, dishonesty, and outright theft were permanent fixtures of many Soviet workplaces.

Dedushka Misha hated the corruption. He would complain to Mama "Thieves are everywhere. Sasha steals from Yuri and Yuri steals from the department next door and so on." He was always looking for a more ethical place to work. He moved from job to job, but in the end he'd realize that the new place was filled with as many thieves as the one before.

Slowly and painfully, my grandfather let go of his dreams of a just Soviet world, and of owning his own small piece of land. But there was one dream that would not let him rest.

One winter day, Dedushka Misha and I were sitting at the blue kitchen table in our apartment while the snow whispered against the window. He watched me running my fingers lightly over the bumpy skin of an orange. Oranges were scarce, and when Mama found some, Natasha and I would each get one, while my parents shared theirs. "Tinochka, do you like oranges?" asked my grandfather.

"Of course," I said. "If I could, I would eat a hundred of them!"

"You know, there is a place where orange trees line the streets. All you have to do is say that you would like to go there with me, and you can pick them yourself."

"Where?" The thought was thrilling.

"Israel! It is a country for Jewish people. Your Mama, Papa, and Natasha will surely join us later." The possibility made me proud. Out of Dedushka's four grandchildren, I was the lucky one to be selected for this impossible adventure. I would have gone anywhere with him. Except to Israel. It was a word I could not even say out loud to my friends, Susanna, Olga, and Galina. They would not have understood. They would have stopped talking to me, or would have whispered about me behind my back.

Instead of giving Dedushka the answer he longed for, I asked him to help me with the orange's thick, stubborn skin. I watched him peel the orange for me and put the sections on a plate. When I offered him a piece, he refused.

Dedushka presented his idea to Mama. Mama would not hear a word of it. After that, he never brought up the subject again.

That spring, Mama and I tried, as usual, to plant petunias in the small wooden flower boxes on our balcony. Dedushka praised my efforts, telling me that I had golden hands and that flowers would surely blossom as a result of my efforts. The flowers grew, but in the end they were cruelly shredded by our cat, Shusha, who used the planters as her litter box.

Dedushka Misha would live on in the small apartment on Stretskaya Street for several years after Babushka Bronya died. Until his death in 1978, he remained a foreigner in the country of his birth, reaching the land of Israel only in his dreams.

Years later, I stood in the orchard of a kibbutz in Galilee among hundreds of young orange trees. I picked one and wiped its dusty skin. The juice ran down my fingers, hands, and elbows. I saluted Dedushka's memory, choking on my tears. I closed my eyes to the rising sun and bit into the orange's tangy flesh.

The straps of her white sandals were almost invisible in the folds of her swollen ankles, tiny pearls of sweat beaded on her white forehead and her breath came in strained puffs as Babushka Bronya and I slowly made our way to the bus stop. The morning, long and sunny, turned into a lovely gentle afternoon as the clouds moved slowly across the sky. It was too early for people to be coming home from work, so the bus that pulled up was almost empty and we could hand our fare directly to the driver. Usually we participated in a minor miracle of Kiev life. The daily rules of corruption and theft didn't apply on the bus, for reasons no one understood. On a crowded public vehicle, your fare could be passed safely from hand to hand until it reached the driver, and your exact change always made its way back to you.

Excited to have a window seat all to myself, I was soon lost in the moving images outside. I awoke with a start to the voice of a woman who kissed Babushka warmly. They settled in for a

Babushka Bronya and Dedushka Misha as I remember them.

good catch-up chat as the bus lurched. They spoke in Yiddish, but I understood when the woman pinched my cheeks and said, "She looks like your youngest."

"She is. She's Svetlana's daughter."

I am not sure if their voices sounded loud in the almost empty bus, or if they really were speaking loudly, but hearing Yiddish outside of home, out in the open, felt like trouble to me. The slightest sign of "Jewishness" – a Jewish name, ethnic features, or a slight accent common among elderly Jews who had trouble pronouncing the long Russian *r* – could land you an ugly stare or a taunt of "Dirty *Zsid*." Young children often called each other *Zsid* at the slightest provocation, whether or not one of them was actually Jewish. The word was meant to be a painful insult.

Sitting a few rows ahead, a middle-aged Ukrainian woman in a colorful print dress and a necklace of plastic beads, held a string bag overflowing with soil-flecked green onions and radishes. She turned around and threw us a hostile look. Babushka and her friend did not notice, but I did. It made me afraid. I tugged

Babushka's arm. Thinking that I was bored or wanting attention, she absently stroked my head.

The woman turned again, and this time she spoke. "Just look at them talking! We do not speak that language in Ukraine. If you want to speak Jewish, get out of here and go to Israel!"

Grandmother and her friend looked at each other and then lowered their eyes as if they had been caught stealing. Babushka's friend murmured, "They want us dead."

Nobody spoke up for us. The other Russian and Ukrainian passengers quickly looked away. Some of them may have agreed with the woman. More than likely, they just didn't want to get involved. There were one or two other Jews on the bus and they also glared accusingly at Babushka and her friend for breaking the cardinal rule: Stay invisible.

The vinyl seat burned my legs and sent uncomfortable warm flushes all the way to my face. Babushka composed herself and tried her best to restore the normalcy of our outing. "When we get home, I will make you tea and *blinchike* with cheese." I said nothing. I didn't want tea or cheese blinchike. What I wanted was to disappear; to erase what had just happened.

The bus stopped at Stretskaya Street. We got out. Babushka didn't see the second attack coming any more than she noticed the first one. This time, it came from me. My cheeks burning and my voice trembling, I said, "Babushka, don't ever speak Yiddish outside again! It makes me embarrassed."

Babushka's shoulders slumped as if someone had landed a blow on them. She let go of my hand and looked away. With a strange longing, she watched the bus drive off as if it carried someone she loved.

We walked the rest of the way to her apartment on Stretskaya Street, toward the place where Mama and Papa fell in love, where my sister and I took our first steps, and where there was an old cemetery among the trees. We plodded silently along, but in the opposite direction to the Jews who had marched to their death at Babi Yar.

I have never forgotten the quality and weight of my grandmother's silence as we drank our evening tea and I played my fork over the blinchike she made for me that night. As I watched the sugar cube melt in the amber of my tea glass, our usual comfortable conversation was absent. I forgot the song I had sung to her earlier that day. Each of us was quiet, lost in our own thoughts, as we got ready for bed.

As she always did when I stayed over, Babushka Bronya laid out a white, starched nightgown she had sewn for me out of good cotton. She handed me her large toothed comb and, moving slowly, she unrolled her long, gray braid. I combed her hair more gently than ever that night. Outside I could smell Dedushka's lilac bushes, their tiny blossoms shivering in the soft evening breeze.

I knew I had hurt my grandmother much more than the Ukrainian woman on the bus ever could have, but I could not apologize. My shame was greater than my love for her.

Babushka Bronya died later that year, soon after I had turned eleven. She died, lying on the bed where I'd combed her hair, looking out the window at Dedushka Misha's lilac trees. Even now, the scent of lilacs carried by a soft spring breeze brings her face to me.

My grandfather, Misha, holding baby Natasha on Stretskaya Street.

Babushka Bronya holding me a few years later.

STRETSKAYA STREET

Dedushka planted his lilacs and peonies the first year that he and Babushka Bronya moved back to Kiev from Uzbekestan, where they had fled during World War II. Kiev had been occupied and most of the buildings destroyed. They were given housing in the same building as Babushka Inna. They had a room in one of the communal apartments and dorms that were only meant to house people until the country was rebuilt.

But thirty-five years after the war, thousands of people like my grandparents, people who had no connections in the government or money to bribe crooked officials, were still living in these crowded dwellings. My grandparents' building had no phone, no hot water, and no private showers. As soon as you walked in you were whacked by a mixture of sounds and smells that were not in the least contained by the cardboard walls: a baby crying, a radio newscast turned up too loud, coughing, arguments, and laughter. It was impossible to identify the odors. They were an ever-changing brew of fried onions and fish, overripe garbage, and urine.

A long corridor dissected the first floor, and on either side were one-room units. Bikes, large and small, boxes of books, rolled-up carpets, and old bed frames lined each side of the hallway as if they had escaped the overcrowded rooms and their frustrated residents.

Living so tightly packed together was not all bad. If you had a baby at home and needed milk, there was always someone to keep an eye on the child for you, or better yet, to fetch the milk. Loneliness and solitude were non-existent. They were luxurious concepts that one heard about only in Russian novels and songs.

The cooking arrangements were a special torment for Babushka Bronya. Two kitchens serviced the whole floor. In each one, a couple of stoves and tables were meant to be shared by all the residents. A stove had four burners and every family was allocated one burner of its own. If anyone needed to use an extra burner, it had to be with the permission of the primary user.

This was the source of much conflict. "Who can make a meal over one burner?" Babushka would wonder. "I have to go and beg again!" If a person did not want to ask a neighbor for the use of her burner, she had to become an expert on the comings and goings of that person, learning when she got up, left for work, or went to bed. A miscalculation always ended in a nasty fight.

Babushka had the misfortune to share her stove with Luska, an old woman who lived alone down the hall. Luska and Babushka had profound and irreconcilable differences. When Luska passed by in the narrow corridor, a plume of pungent odor, a mixture of sweat and food, trailed after her. When she fried her fish, she saw no need, nor had any desire to open the kitchen window. She didn't care if the entire floor was filled with the stench of her oily dinner. The grease splattered everywhere, dirtying the wall behind the burner and the floor around the stove.

I often wondered what made Luska so mean. Maybe it was because her husband went away to war and when he returned, it was not to her but to someone else – somewhere else. Or perhaps it was because one day a train went through her village station, taking with it a chunk of her leg as she tried to cross the tracks. Whether it was the injury to her heart or her leg, she had been left bitter and angry. Babushka was convinced that if she left her soup pot unattended longer than a minute, Luska was so mean that she might spit or even pee in it.

The idea of it was frightening to me. I tried to imagine Luska reaching for a chair to climb onto the stove and perch over the pot. I comforted myself with the thought that in such a crowded building, a person would have to be quick and spry to accomplish the terrible deed, and Luska, with her heavy limp, was neither.

A small chicken coup for the neighbors' chickens, built from scraps of old wood, sat outside the building's dirty kitchen windows. Luska's chickens were as obnoxious as their mistress. Given a hint of opportunity, they always made their way into the kitchen to look for food, warmth, or a little adventure. Babushka said that she saw Luska's hate for her in those chicken eyes. I tried never to look at Luska, but when I couldn't help it, I could see that her eyes *were* like her birds' – tiny beads, shiny and dark.

Luska's hens were always being shushed out into the backyard, and it gave me a particular pleasure to chase them. Like Luska, they also left a trail – of droppings and feathers. Even though my grandmother disliked her neighbor and the chickens, she found their feathers useful. I gathered them up, rinsed them thoroughly, and tied them in bundles. When I baked with Babushka, we used those feathers to brush *piroshky* (dumplings filled with meat, cherries, or apples) with melted butter, before they went into the oven.

The chickens had been part of Stretskaya Street forever. When their predecessors were eaten, a new, identical generation appeared, making them seem eternal.

Stretskaya was a modest, ordinary street, but it had been the scene of many small joys and of immense sorrows. Stretskaya was the street where my parents had met and fallen in love as children, and where Natasha and I had taken our first steps. It was also the street on which Nazis led thousands of Jews to their death at Babi Yar.

Stripped of their documents, valuables, and clothes, they were marched to the edge of the ravine at gunpoint and shot to death. After their bodies fell into the mass grave, they were buried by earth brought in to cover the horrid deed. Under the fresh earth, emaciated children's bodies lay crooked, like broken dolls, over the naked bodies of their mothers, who clutched them in a final embrace.

Time had covered the communal grave with lush grass. Even a few trees had managed to take root.

When Papa returned to Kiev as a young teenager after the Nazis were defeated, he and his rebellious friends often gathered and biked at the edge of that ravine, and would see teeth and bones – silent witnesses to these crimes. Despite the years that had passed, the place still resembled an earthen mouth forever open in a silent scream.

Everyone knew what had happened at Babi Yar, but few dared to talk about. In Kiev, where a monument to Soviet heroism and victory over the Nazis decorated every possible corner, this site remained without a marker for decades.

Just up the hill lay an old cemetery covered by rich green bushes and grass, where Jews and Christians were buried in separate sections. At some point the cemetery was declared full and was closed to new graves, but family members and loved ones continued to make their way up the overgrown path, past the rusty iron gate, to pay their respects to the dead.

A handful of old people who had nothing to lose, either because they were brave or because they no longer cared, risked arrest and possibly deportation to Siberia by daring to recite *kaddish* at the graves. For the surviving Jews of Kiev, they became the source, the memory bank, of all that was left of Judaism. People who knew they were Jewish, but who had nobody to teach them what that meant, would come to the cemetery to pose whispered questions to these old people: When does Rosh Hashanah fall this year? Who is baking matzo for Passover this year? What are the rituals for burying a loved one?

Any religious expression – Christian, Jewish, or Muslim – was strongly discouraged by the Soviets. The few surviving churches that were open to the public served as museums, as much as places of worship. The clergy were strictly supervised by the Soviet state. During Easter, midnight masses were held at Kiev's splendid historical churches, and defiant worshippers holding lit candles flocked to pray. But teachers from school were stationed at the doors to watch for the faces of their students.

The next morning pupils who had been seen attending services were summoned to appear in front of the student body and to face criticism and public shaming. The next step was often expulsion and possibly a ruined life.

Despite the rules, during Orthodox Easter my Russian and Ukrainian classmates sometimes brought fluffy, sweet pastries called *babka* and colorfully painted eggs to school, prepared lovingly by unlikely enemies of the state – their grandmothers. Every spring without fail, a few pieces of matzo made their humble appearance in the deepest recess of our kitchen cupboard. I never asked how they came to be in there. Something deep inside me prevented me from wanting to know any details.

I never took the matzo to school. If I were caught, it would mean a public shaming, and the idea of public disgrace terrified me. So I munched on matzo in the safety of our small living room, far away from Stretskaya Street, and wondered why my Russian and Ukrainian friends had much prettier and sweeter treats from their not-so-distant religious past.

THE DANCERS

I BALANCED ON THE WOODEN STOOL BY THE KITCHEN WINDOW AND PEERED INTO PAPA'S SHAVING MIRROR. I FLIPPED IT FROM THE MAGNIFYING SIDE TO THE NORMAL ONE AND BROUGHT MY FACE closer. "Yich . . . I hate you!"

They stared back at me defiantly. All seven of them. They had settled on my forehead, cheeks, and nose and by the look of them, they weren't about to budge.

If I was going to grab my big chance at romance, I would have to declare war on each of those seven detestable red, bumpy pimples.

I planned my campaign with every possible weapon available to a thirteen-year-old girl in Kiev, where so many basics were hard to find, much less such luxuries as acne treatments. A good face scrub with soap and water, a gentle dabbing with a towel, and then the heaviest gun: *zelonka.* The bright green disinfectant that smelled like alcohol, applied with a bit of cotton wrapped around the tip of one of Papa's matches, would do the trick. Then all I'd need was time to hide. I knew that if I left the zelonka on my face for at least a day, my enemies would shrink and I would emerge from battle ready to greet the New Year, victorious and smooth-skinned.

There was no time to waste. It was only a few days before New Year's Eve, a time when the whole country celebrated. Families and friends would gather around a late-night dinner table to eat platters of cold fish, potato salad, and chopped liver. They would turn on the television for the midnight concert broadcast from Moscow, and drink and dance until dawn. That was the best part: more than anything in the world, I loved to dance.

Up until then, I'd been an enthusiastic, if solitary dancer. Every day when I got home from school, I hurried to draw the curtains, turn on the record player, and imagine that our small living room was a bright stage. I only had a few precious minutes of time alone – soon my parents or Natasha would arrive and preparations for dinner would start – so I didn't

Tchaikovsky's earth-bound swan, practicing in the woods.

waste a minute changing from my school uniform. In my brown dress, black apron, and red pioneer scarf I became Tchaikovsky's lonely swan, Prokofiev's star-crossed Juliet, or Bizet's passionate Carmen. I waltzed, I was seduced, and I died a tragic, graceful death in the narrow space between the yellow, plastic-covered sofa and the chestnut buffet.

Lately, my solitary matinee performances had begun to bore me. I was tired of dancing alone. I longed to dance with a partner, and New Year's held that promise in the form of Boris.

Boris's parents and mine had been friends as long as I could remember. He was everything I was not. He was, to say the least, serious. Boris spent hours playing the piano or pouring over a chessboard with his father, the veins protruding through the thin skin of his temples, as he considered his next move. Boris read everything in sight. He seldom spoke, and when he did, he was brutally honest. I had never seen him smile. Mama said that his sense of humor was like an arrow: precise, cruel, and sharp.

I was the opposite of the self-contained Boris. I often felt like the champagne bottle Papa had opened last New Year's Eve. It had fizzed up and spilled all over the table, uncontrollable, bubbly. We had laughed then, but it wasn't easy at all to be like a champagne bottle: effervescent, explosive, and exposed. I wondered how Boris could hold so much inside.

From the time that we were children, our families had shared many holidays and outings to the countryside to search for mushrooms and to pick hazelnuts or berries, but it wasn't until a hot August day that I actually became aware of Boris as a boy. We were sitting on the trunk of a fallen tree during the mushroom hunt, waiting for our parents to catch up to us. I chatted. Boris sat silently, studying the toes of his boots. Suddenly he lifted his curly eyelashes, looked up at me as if he was seeing me for the first time, and said, "You smile a lot, and when you do, your dimples are uneven." I wasn't sure if it was a compliment or a criticism. I looked away, a warm glow spreading over my cheeks and through the rest of me.

"At least I smile, which is something you never do."

Boris threw me a quick glance, got up, and walked down the path. His silence infuriated me and I sensed that the last word would be his.

The plans for New Year's Eve had been made months ago. In a country where religion was forbidden, we poured all our anticipation and heart into New Year's celebrations. This year was our turn to play host.

I could imagine every thrilling minute of it: Papa would dance with Mama, holding her gently and awkwardly. Boris's mother, Bella, would clutch her husband, Yasha, to her ample body and lead him around the room to nostalgic Russian songs. ("I loved you. You left. You came back again and now I am in charge.") That would leave Boris and me to sit together on the sofa, and instead of pretending we had no interest in dancing together, this New Year's would be different. No verbal punches would be thrown or caught, no uncomfortable bursts of laughter would build a wall between us. Boris would stand up and straighten his back. He would look right at me, take my hand, and with an elegant swoop, he would draw me close to him . . .

All that stood in the way were seven ugly pimples that, by exerting great effort and restraint, I had not squeezed.

I took a deep breath, dipped the cotton-covered match into the zelonka, and set to work with surgical precision. These were desperate measures, but a clear-faced New Year's was worth it. Staring back from the mirror was a girl with her hair scraped back by a black headscarf, and her face marked with seven vivid green dots. "*Oy, oy nu ea Pugalo!* What a scary crow!" I stuck my tongue out. I put my father's shaving mirror back on the kitchen shelf, turned off the light, and glanced out the window at the walkway, three storeys below.

The snowdrifts looked like the folds of a large purple fur coat. A fragment of a phrase or the tail end of a laugh from the few people hurrying home sounded muffled and soft. Soon there would be the stillness and peace of a Kiev winter night. Peaceful for some, but not for me, as it turned out.

We actually had one of Kiev's rare telephones. Mama had stood in line and paid a bribe, so our name had moved up the list. Eventually the phone was installed, but it had been out of order for a week now. (In my opinion it was a sign of a just world, because Natasha laid claim to it for hours at a time. I had nobody to call. My friends did not have telephones. But still.) Repairmen had been called, but had not materialized.

Because there were so few phones, and even fewer working ones, and because mail was likely to be opened by censors, most messages, no matter how trivial, had to be delivered in person. Even telling somebody that you wanted to meet for a stroll in the park on Wednesday instead of Thursday could mean a long bus ride preceded by an even longer wait for a bus.

The hardship was made less so by turning the relay of a message into a social event. It was not unusual for friends and neighbors to drop in on each other unexpectedly and to stay for a visit and a cup of tea. Normally I would be the first to run and open the door at any sign of visitors, but normally I did not have seven large green dots on my face. So, when I heard someone knock at our door, I sensed danger.

I heard Papa opening the door, the exchange of kisses, and voices raised in enthusiastic greeting. Voices I was not expecting to hear until New Year's Eve. Voices I most certainly did not *want* to hear, while standing in a two-room apartment where there was no place to hide the fact that I had a face dotted with seven green spots. All of a sudden, the world seemed less just. The voices belonged to Bella, Yasha, and Boris. They had a message for us and had taken the bus across the city to deliver it. I bit my lip and flattened myself against the kitchen sink, in the futile hope that they would pay their visit and leave without noticing that I was there.

The clinking of wine glasses suggested that they were staying. In the low light I stared at the dirty dishes piled in the sink. In a desperate attempt to avoid being noticed, I turned on the water. I watched the thin stream move toward the drain, taking with it scraps of onion, carrot peel, and cabbage. I wanted to be small enough to float away with what was left of dinner. I was ready to give up the New Year's celebrations and my dance with Boris – anything – if I could only be spared the humiliation of being caught with a face marked by Seven Green Enemies (or red ones if I could have managed to get the persistent zelonka off, which was next to impossible until it dried). I closed my eyes and waited for a miracle. Instead, I heard Mama calling me. "Tinochka, we have guests!"

There was no escape. I entered the living room feeling sick. Afraid to look up, I mumbled hello to Bella. She added a red lipstick kiss to the green polka dots on my face.

Reprieve. Boris had his back to me, looking through the books on the bookshelf, as usual. This time there was enough to hold his attention. We'd acquired something rare and precious. Two new volumes of Sholom Aleichem's short stories sat on our shelves.

The books came to us from a grateful patient of my Aunt Rima who had arranged for the family to have a special subscription to The Library of the World's Greatest Writers, a collection of beautifully illustrated, well-bound books by the best of the world's writers and poets. In a country where so many books were forbidden or out of reach, this was a gift of unimaginable worth.

Every month a notice arrived in the mail, announcing that a new book had come. If we didn't pick it up on time, it would be sold to someone else.

We were camping in the countryside, when by some miracle, notice reached us that the collection of stories by Sholom Aleichem was waiting for us in Kiev. Quickly, we packed our tent, deflated our mattresses, and put out our lively fire. What were a few days of vacation in exchange for two volumes of Sholom Aleichem?

Sholom Aleichem was Jewish, but the Soviet censors approved his work anyway, because it served their purposes to do so. He was a brilliant satirist. He depicted the life of the prerevolutionary shtetl in the bleak colors of poverty and injustice. The stories were supposed to illustrate how bad life had been before communism came along to save us all. But for us, that was beside the point. Through rueful shopkeepers' dialogues, and a milkman's conversations with God, through bearded rabbis' teachings and stories of poor grooms and rich brides, a vanished way of Jewish life breathed again from the pages. His books gave us back the world – destroyed by the Soviet revolution, and then by the Nazis – that was no more.

We reached the book office just in time and the volumes were ours. Now they had pride of place on our bookshelf. I watched as Boris read. His profile looked like one of the heroes in Sholom Aleichem's stories. I bit my lip.

Bella was exploding with the news they'd come to share. They would not be able to see in the New Year with us after all. Boris had qualified for the chess championships that were taking place over the holiday in Moscow. They had brought a bottle of champagne with them to toast the upcoming year tonight and to celebrate Boris's great achievement.

"We are so happy for you! What a pleasant surprise, and what an accomplishment, Borinka!" Mama directed her eyes at me as she spoke, making her point silently: Boris was a serious student and thinker and not a butterfly like she often called me.

Even though it only took Boris a few moments to turn around and face me, many things went through my mind. Why did it take so little for a boy to be attractive when I had to spend so much time in front of the mirror, worrying? Why were some people strong enough to keep their thoughts and feelings to themselves while others had their feelings splashed about, like the salty water of the Black Sea against its rocky shore? And why was it possible for such delicious plans to be crushed with a simple, friendly knock on the door?

Boris's dark brown, penetrating eyes looked me over: the faded housecoat, the scuffed slippers, the black band on my head holding my hair upright, and my green polka-dotted face. He gave me a brief greeting, *privet*. I lowered my head, trying not to show tears, my flushed cheeks, and my terrible disappointment.

I could not stare at the freshly-polished parquet floor forever. Eventually I looked up, and despite my earlier assumptions, I learned that, in fact, Boris had a wide and warm smile.

Part 2

Natasha had plans to spend New Year's with her friends and I was resigned to spending the most important night of the year in the company of adults, but I embellished it with all kinds of fantasies I didn't believe would come true. Nevertheless, that New Year's Eve held its own sweet surprise.

Zina sat across from me at a dining-room table covered with platters of food, china, and delicate crystal glasses filled with ruby-red wine. She was at least fifteen years older than me, but she seemed to think of me as her peer, and directed a stream of questions at me in garbled words I couldn't understand. Despite her mother's attempts to soothe her and control her loud exclamations and flapping hands, her excitement was too much to contain. Not many guests came through the door of this home. Besides, it was a holiday and we were going to stay up all night to witness the old year change into the new. The holiday and the visitors were an intoxicating brew for Zina.

Zina lived with her elderly mother, her married sister, Masha, and Masha's husband, Isaac Krefetz, in a cramped apartment. We shared bonds. Like us, they were a Jewish family struggling to survive the wearing drudgery of Soviet life. And there was another bond, one that was never discussed. Years earlier, my parents had hidden illegal literature belonging to Isaac's father in our apartment, risking their own safety, and saving the old man from a brutal arrest or exile to a gulag in Siberia.

Masha was a talented physician – the crystal wine glasses that were kept in her heavy breakfront attested to her patients' gratitude. A red oriental carpet was pinned to the wall. Heavy bookcases made the modest room seem even smaller and cozier.

Isaac hung our coats on a hook and before we could sit down, the bedroom door opened slowly. Masha's mother entered. Behind her, holding her mother's hand, was Zina. She had Down syndrome.

Although I was thirteen, it was the first time in my life that I had actually been in the presence of someone with a mental disability. Despite spending much of our lives out in public – walking almost everywhere, standing in food lines, riding city buses – we almost never saw disabled people. When we did see somebody with a physical or mental handicap, we looked away. The country that prided itself on being built on rights and equalities miserably failed its most vulnerable citizens. Disabled people were invisible, untouchables. The vast Soviet Union had no wheelchair access to public buildings and very few schools for people with handicaps. Families were left, isolated and ashamed, to fend for themselves in crowded Soviet apartments.

No wonder Zina was excited to see us. Her only company was her immediate family, so guests were an incredible treat, and a young person was almost unbearably thrilling for her.

I stared at her discreetly across the New Year's table as I used my fork to pick at the head of the stuffed fish on the platter between us. Every time she caught my eye Zina smiled and made loud sounds. Her mother spoke to her softly and translated: Zina wants to know if you go to school. Zina didn't wait for me to answer. She told me that she wanted to go to school, but couldn't. In short order I learned that she liked listening to the news on the radio, eating boiled potatoes, and that the walkway to their apartment complex was full of snow. For Zina, things connected and made sense in ways that were not obvious to me. That night Zina had found the closest thing to a friend she had ever had, and perhaps ever would have, and she was not about to let the opportunity slip away.

When the dishes were cleared Masha served the dessert Mama had made, baked puffs filled with heavenly vanilla cream. Zina and I exchanged conspiratorial looks as we took them apart and licked the cream from each half. Then we settled in front of the small television with its long antenna ears to watch a potpourri of comedians, poets, opera singers, and dancers televised from Moscow right across the Soviet Union.

A handsome singer came on stage and sang a song, lyrical and beautiful, that seemed to flow from the small screen to fill the warm room. It was the kind of song that makes you dream of dancing close to someone you love. Holding the shell of a cream puff in my hand, I closed my eyes and listened to the melody, lost in fantasies of Boris: Boris, his game of chess, my newly smooth complexion, my soft blue dress swirling as we spun across the floor. Soon I was asleep.

I felt someone's warm breath on my face. I opened my eyes and met the eager gaze of slanted brown eyes.

"Dance. You. Me. Dance. Good to dance," said Zina. I tried to understand. Does she want me to dance with her? Zina had not been part of my dance fantasy.

I looked around. The room was empty of adults. They were in the kitchen talking as they cleaned up. Nobody was going to save me.

"Dance," she insisted. "You. Me. Dance!" She took my hand in her plump rough-skinned one and pulled me into the small open space near the table. She was wearing a simple gray wool dress, and on her legs were thick brown stockings that disappeared into the velvet slippers on her big feet. She closed her eyes and began to move.

Zina let go of my hand and stretched her arms into the air. At first her movements were clumsy and awkward and had nothing to do with the flow of the song. There must have been other music – her own music – playing just for her. I watched her tilt her head back and move her arms as if she were a tree touched by an autumn wind. Her arm movements changed, and now she was a bird looking for a place to light. She did not care if she looked clumsy or funny. Breathing heavily, Zina danced for her own pleasure. What she was, was free.

We must have made an unusual pair. Me, in my new, blue dress (actually Natasha's dress remade for me by Mama), twirling and spinning, dancing with Zina, heavy-footed, awkward, and joyful. I could only imagine what Boris would have made of this scene.

The music stopped and the TV hostess announced the next performance, but Zina continued to dance. She stopped only when she was ready to stop. When she opened her eyes, she and I bowed to the imaginary audience, and when we realized our families were watching us from the kitchen doorway, we howled with laughter.

By the end of the evening, I could understand some of Zina's cryptic speech and I needed less and less of her mother's help. When the time came to say good-bye that snowy New Year's night, Papa helped Mama and me with our coats and we made our way to the door. My parents thanked the Krefetzes for a wonderful evening and we all kissed and hugged. At the entryway, I turned around and caught sight of Zina's face, peering at me from behind her mother.

As I raised my hand to wave to her, I met Zina's warm, shiny gaze. She winked at me like one friend to another, once they have shared a secret.

I would happily have died for my handsome papa.

THE PUSHKIN LOVER

MAMA WAS BENT OVER THE BATHTUB. HER STRONG, FAST HANDS FISHED FOR THE SHEETS AND TOWELS THAT FLOATED IN THE SOAPY WATER. SKILLFULLY SHE LIFTED HER CATCH AND RAN IT OVER THE wavy surface of the washboard. The sounds she made reminded me of shutters rattling in the cold winter winds.

There was no space in the bathroom for both of us, so I stood in the doorway, holding my notebook. I could hear children in the courtyard below. They were counting and laughing as they skipped rope. Although I'd soon be fourteen, and almost too old for childish play, I longed to be outside with them, but I didn't dare move.

"Read me what you've written. I'm listening," Mama said, barely lifting her head from the washing. Mama had been awarded the red diploma in early childhood education, the highest possible honor, and she believed that her daughters needed more challenge than school could offer. Not a day passed without her assigning us something to write.

Sometimes I'd complain to Papa as he lay in his usual position, stretched out on the sofa reading *Pravda*. He'd lower his newspaper and his brown tender eyes would plead with me: "Please Tinochka, do it for me this one time. You don't want to get me into trouble, do you?"

Get him in trouble? I would die for him. Just last summer when we were camping on the bank of the Desna, an arm of the Dnieper River, he took me fishing with him. We stood near the water and cast our lines. In no time Papa had a bite and reeled in a large, stubborn fish that fought all the way to the riverbank. Suddenly, inches from where I was standing, it broke free. Papa yelled, "Tinka, lovey. Catch!" thinking that I would reach out and grab the fish. Instead, without a thought, I bolted after the fish into the cold, fast-running water. Papa pulled me out, but we lost our catch. When he delivered me to Mama shivering and soaked, she was furious.

"Are you crazy?" she yelled at him. "It's been raining for days and she has no dry clothes to wear!"

I was frozen, but strangely happy as she tucked me into a sleeping bag and told Papa he had lost his mind. Then she hung my wet clothes over the fire to dry.

"Of course I don't want to get you in trouble," I whispered to Papa and went back to Mama with the composition she had assigned. Today's subject was "The Arrival of an Early Spring." I had to create an outline and fill it in with observations of the changes in nature around me.

Mama wasted no time while I read to her. A large pot of soup was simmering on the stove in the kitchen and its aroma mixed with the smell of harsh soap. She scrubbed at clothes in the tub, her back so bowed that her corrections sounded like they were coming from below the surface of the ocean. I could see the silver metal rollers in Mama's hair. Although the streets were still wet from a dirty, late snow, streaked like mascara on the face of an unhappy woman, the rollers that would assure Mama of "the look" she wanted for tomorrow, were a definite sign of spring. Tomorrow was March 8, International Women's Day.

Every March 8, the Soviet Union toasts and celebrates the accomplishments, contributions, and charms of women. Husbands and sons, brothers and grandsons, do the cooking and serving to honor all the women in their lives. (Even though we were supposed to do the cooking for this special day, Mama was a realist. She knew her family's limitations and she always made the dinner herself.) Women celebrate other women too. Daughters bring their mothers flowers and gifts and write them cards of appreciation and gratitude.

Last year Papa had given Natasha and me kerchiefs for Women's Day. Natasha's was white with blue polka dots. Mine was white with red polka dots. I loved putting it on because it felt so light and spring-like after months with my head buried under my heavy winter hat.

Finding the right Women's Day gift for Mama was never easy. She didn't like clutter, knickknacks, or perfume. Flowers made her happy, but finding fresh flowers on the eve of March 8 was impossible, unless you knew someone in a flower shop, or someone who knew someone who did. The usual.

Mama and I had spent from early afternoon until early evening the day before International Women's Day standing in line. The line began in the store, but it soon grew until it had wrapped itself around the block like a snake with a long wavy tail. Mama asked the man in front of us: "What are they selling here?"

This was not an unusual question. It was not uncommon to join a line without knowing what was being sold. Whatever it was, most likely we didn't have it. If we did have it, we were probably about to run out of it. If neither was the case, then someone in the family or a friend likely needed it. Lining up was a way of life.

"I'm not sure myself," he said. "At first the word was that it was toilet paper, but I haven't seen anybody carrying any out of the store. Then I heard it was oranges. Now I think it's canned fish. Salmon, I hope." The man sighed. "It helps to know someone. Without connections life is impossible."

Both Mama and the stranger understood what "connections" meant. "Connections" meant you didn't have to stand in line and wait for hours in the cold. You could go to the back of the store and have a salesclerk bring out items that would never appear on display or for sale. It meant that you could have a holiday table full of food, even though the shelves in the grocery stores were empty. It meant that you could apply to the university of your choice, and be accepted on the grounds that a member of the faculty happened to owe one of your relatives a favor. "Connections" meant that the cramped quarters you shared with three other families could be exchanged for a small, private space for your family alone. And if one of your loved ones was ill, "connections" meant getting into the hospital and onto the operating table sooner than those who died in the hallways waiting for a surgeon – like my Papa's cousin Mitya had. People with connections dressed better.

"Connections" meant that just possibly you could beat the impossible system.

"Fish would be good on the table," said Mama. The man turned around to face the back of the woman in front of him, who was standing behind someone else.

Efficient, organized Mama was not one to waste endless hours standing in line. "Tinochka," she began, and by the tone of her voice I knew that a new study initiative was about to be put into action. "What are you studying in Literature this week?"

I was happy to answer. I loved Literature, and it was one of the few subjects I did well in. "Pushkin, *Ruslan and Ludmilla*."

"Tell me what you've learned about it." Mama sounded pleased.

Pushkin was a national treasure and everyone knew his life story. He'd been born in Moscow in 1799, to an old boyar family. His maternal grandfather, Ibraham Hannibal, was supposed to have been an Abyssinian prince. In 1705, a Russian envoy found him living as a hostage at the court of a Turkish sultan and took the boy back to St. Petersburg as a gift to the czar, Peter the Great. His grandson's life was almost as romantic. Not yet forty years old, Pushkin the poet died in a duel, defending his wife's honor. His huge gambling debts were paid by none other than Czar Nicholas I.

Pushkin was a true romantic and a favorite of Mama's and mine.

In his short life Pushkin composed poems, fairy tales, and prose. The elegant, yet simple language, the heroes, and the descriptions of lush country landscape were the very best of classical Russian culture. The dreamy images, witty language, and strong stories allowed readers an easy entry into the fantastic worlds he created. No wonder so many adults could reach into their memories and recite the Pushkin verses they had learned as children.

Sarah Yosipovna, our Russian Language and Literature teacher, had taught us *Ruslan and Ludmilla*, Pushkin's masterpiece, in a voice little more than a whisper as she bent her body conspiratorially over her desk. "There, in that magical world, an oak tree stood on a curved seashore," she said. "A mermaid sat in its branches and a wise cat walked back and forth along a golden chain wrapped around the oak. The learned cat sang songs and told tales, and one of them was the story of the lovers Ruslan and Ludmilla who were separated and then united."

The line inched forward. "We're supposed to memorize a passage," I told Mama.

"Why don't you practice reciting it now?" said Mama. "It looks like we'll be here for awhile."

Reciting poetry from memory was a common pastime, the mark of a learned person. Even though a fine education didn't buffer anybody from the harsh daily problems of Soviet life (it was common to meet highly educated people working way below their skill level in order to feed their families) the ability to "own" a poem by memorizing it, was a highly respected skill.

We all shuffled forward a few steps and I stepped out of line to gauge the amount of line-time left. If I recited for Mama, I wouldn't have to study later.

I took a deep breath and began to recite Pushkin's lush verses, but Mama interrupted me. "Do it with expression. You are not reading a newspaper."

I recited some more, but paused for a moment, letting my attention stray to a little white dog a young girl led on a leash. The man in front of us turned around and took up where I had left off: "... and the wise black cat walked upon the golden chain that circled the ancient oak." He had fierce brows, an old scar marking his cheek, and a dark cap pulled down over his eyes. But his face was radiant as he recited. "I loved these verses and still remember them from my childhood," he explained. We finished the poem together.

Mama smiled at him. "You must have been a good student. See," she looked at me pointedly, "a good education stays with you forever."

Papa was a die-hard romantic and was all for me buying flowers for Mama on March 8. Without moving from his kitchen chair where he was sipping his morning tea, he gestured to his coat and told me to take what I needed. The coins stowed in my pocket,

Papa was all in favor of me buying flowers for Mama.

I slipped out of the apartment and made my way out to the sleepy street. The neighborhood was empty except for a few men carrying groceries and packages for the day's celebration.

I filled my lungs with early morning air and walked down the chestnut-tree alley to Vushgorodskaya Street. At the corner stood a small flower shop, a wooden booth, really, with its back to a tall iron fence behind which were state gardens and two large greenhouses. I hoped that the booth was open and that I wasn't too late.

My heart beat faster as I approached the corner, but to my delight I could see a line of people, all of them men, standing on the wet bits of soil that dotted the pavement around the flower booth. By the redness of their cheeks I could tell that they had been there for some time, probably before the booth had even opened.

I was proud to join them. But the line was quite long, and after awhile I began to worry. What if all the flowers were sold by the time my turn came? As I stood in line, moving forward step by slow step, I realized that I wished Mama was with me. She knew how to manage the worst of lines. She knew how to bargain with the market women who tried to sell her vegetables at high prices. She knew how to scan the line ahead for anyone we knew, in case they could help us or give us vital information. She knew how to conquer the wearing boredom. Alone, I felt grown up, but I missed Mama's confident presence.

I watched the men pay in turn and leave the booth, one by one, carrying bouquets of flowers in their arms. A few of them even had two bouquets. *How unfair,* I thought. Some households would get two bouquets and some wouldn't have even one.

The thought of going home without flowers for Mama was awful. Even though her strict rules often chaffed and angered me, I understood how fiercely she loved us. By the time we woke up, she would have spent a couple of hours studying. "My head is fresher in the morning," she explained. She would braid Natasha's and my hair and tie bows around the ends while we lay on our sides in bed. She had our morning omelet ready before she went to work. At the end of the day, after food lines and dinner, there was homework to oversee, sewing or knitting. Her laughter was loud and clear. I knew I would never have the words to tell Mama all the things she deserved to hear. All I wanted to do was to beat the system just this once and make Mama happy by bringing her something beautiful to warm the cold, early spring.

Finally, there were only two more people ahead of me, and then just one man. He stepped up to the kiosk. I heard him grumble. "I've been waiting all this time, and now they're sold out. How am I going to tell my wife, yet again, that I have no flowers for her mother?" He growled at the man in the booth, waved a dismissive hand, and left the line.

I could not go home without flowers. I took a deep breath and approached the small wooden counter. The flower seller had not closed the wooden shutters yet, but he was mopping the floor of the booth and picking up stems and bits of broken greenery.

I tried to sound firm like Mama. "*Tovarisch*, friend, are you sure that there are no flowers left for my mother today?"

He turned to face me. I recognized the brows, the scar on the left cheek and the dark cap. And he recognized me. "The Pushkin lover!" He smiled. "What are you doing up so early? Isn't this Woman's Day? Your brother should be buying you flowers."

I would have returned his smile, but I was so disappointed at the thought of going home empty-handed that I couldn't make my face obey. "I have no brother," I said, "but I wanted to get flowers for my mother, and now I am too late." I looked away, trying not to cry. It was the morning of March 8 and I was a child without any connections.

"Cheer up. I saved a few blooms for my wife. I'll share them with you." He lifted a metal bucket that was almost empty. Water sloshed around on the bottom. I chose five white calla lilies, partially open, long and elegant. He wrapped them in white paper. "I hope your mother enjoys them," he said. "Remember Pushkin. He is the greatest Russian poet."

"*Spasibo Bolshow. Escho Spasibo.* Thank you, thank you very much." As I walked home, my hands nearly frozen, I held the callas' delicate stems carefully as their graceful heads and fine dancers' necks peeked out from the edges of the paper. Several times someone stopped me to ask where I had found such lovely flowers. I was proud to explain. "Unfortunately, they were sold out, but I had connections."

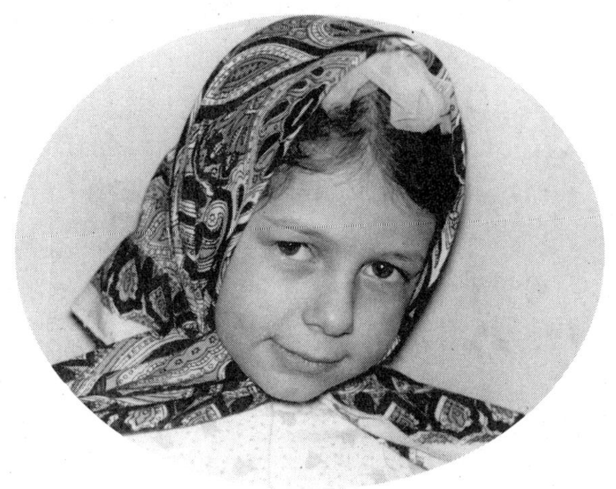

Old Guard in training.

THE OLD GUARD

YOU COULD BARELY SEE THE WOODEN BENCH BENEATH THE SHAPELESS, HEAVILY CLAD BODIES. NO LONGER CONCERNED WITH THE MATTERS OF YOUTH OR BEAUTY, THE WOMEN SAT, STOOPED AND tired, under the generous branches of the chestnut trees in the courtyard. If you looked at them from the back, you might think they were identical. A group of women wearing long-vested jackets and dark scarves – after a certain age they all began to look alike.

They had had fleeting acquaintance with dentistry when they were young, and now in old age their mouths were filled, at best, with gold – at second-best, with silver. The corners of their kerchiefs were tied in wings that flapped under their chins and trembled when they spoke. Tired breasts rested on heavy bellies. Thick, brown stockings encased thick ankles and felt slippers stretched around swollen feet.

Don't confuse them with sweet little old ladies. If you were to take on any one of them, you would have to wrestle the entire team. Better to give them their due, because they rarely forgot and almost never forgave those who crossed them. They were the Old Guard of Krasnapolskay Street.

The Old Guard chewed and spat out gossip with their sunflower seeds. In confidential whispers they would ask each other: "Did you see that young Lydia's new boyfriend?" "Have you heard that Stepan and Rayza's good-for-nothing son is back?" "Who would have thought?" Wishes and longing and sometimes curses were ever on their tongues, tongues that could sting like whips and leave scars for life. They fought amongst themselves. They made up. They fought some more.

Everyone in our apartment building knew everyone else, and there were few secrets that stayed secret. If someone argued with their spouse the night before, we'd know how the fight turned out when the sounds from their bedroom changed to romantic laughter. If a husband's drunkenness put his wife in danger, the other men – including Papa – would make it their duty to remove the offender and sober him up before he was returned to his home.

The Old Guard of Krasnapolskay Street, the babushkas, were the village elders. They had outlived their husbands by at least a decade. They had survived day after weary day of Soviet life. Most of them lived with their grown children, washing, cooking, and looking after the younger grandchildren. In a society where both men and women worked, they were a necessary component of Soviet family life, and their attentions didn't stop at their own grandchildren. Even when they were not on the bench, we knew that critical eyes watched us from every window and balcony whenever we played outside.

The Old Guard. Don't confuse them with sweet little old ladies.

Years of sizing up every person who came into our apartment building meant that the babushkas not only knew each of us, but they could identify our friends and our extended families. The Old Guard could spot, and judge on the spot, any stranger who wandered into the courtyard. They were our own neighborhood watch – our local *censura*. They offered a strange kind of safety in the oppressive Soviet lack of privacy.

Though the babushkas lived in crowded flats with their families, there was something indescribably lonely about them. And because of that, their bench was a daily source of companionship and entertainment. When one of them died, I would see the others wiping their red withered cheeks with the wings of their kerchiefs. But soon they would be joined by another babushka to replace the one who was lost – as if the mantle of guardianship must not be weakened by anything as trifling as death.

Every family's private life was public, thanks to laundry. Each balcony on Krasnapolskay Street was festooned with clotheslines

When it wasn't laundry day, Papa could enjoy the balcony overlooking Krasnapolskay Street.

and wooden clothespins. Wise homemakers hung their sheets and pillowcases on the exterior lines, leaving unmentionables hidden discreetly on the lines closer to the building. But this wasn't foolproof. Everyone knew when a girl was no longer a child – the wind would blow the laundry's theatrical curtains apart to reveal a pair of nylons or a small brassiere that had never hung there before.

Doing the laundry was backbreaking. Mama would bend over the tub, her hands running rhythmically over the washboard as if it were her own musical instrument. She loved music and often sang, but she said ruefully, "This is the only instrument I've ever played." When the laundry was finished, she sat at the kitchen table, back sore and fingers red, sipping a cup of tea prepared for her by Papa. Papa loved her, but he was not about to learn how to play her musical instrument himself.

One fall day, Mama went to Moscow to help my sister, Natasha, settle into her dormitory for her first year of university. Before she left, Mama washed a huge load of laundry. The wet laundry and I were left in Papa's care. The fresh smell of autumn was in the air. I longed to walk with Irina, my best friend, listening to the fallen leaves crunch under our feet and laughing as we stepped over puddles of rainwater that mirrored the scudding clouds in the sky. I couldn't stay indoors for another moment.

Though the day was chilly, I wasn't ready to wrap myself in my heavy winter cocoon of clothing yet. Instead, I threw on a thin sweater and headed downstairs. As I passed the censura I said a brief hello and rushed toward the street. Suddenly, I heard one of the Old Guard: "Tinochka! Are you in too much of a hurry to put on a pair of warm stockings? What do you think this is, the middle of July?"

The others fell silent to allow her to make her sally.

I longed to be with Irina. The day was short, and I was emboldened because Mama was gone. "What business is this of yours?" I said rudely. "What if I told you that I have no winter stockings to wear?"

A finger stabbed at me. "And whose stockings are hanging up there to dry on your balcony, young lady?"

The babushkas looked like birds on an electric power line – alert and ready to jump to support any member of their flock. They adjusted their kerchiefs to make it easier for their concerned foreheads to express annoyance. I hated this busybody intruding into my stockings, but I knew I was no match for them. Outnumbered, I mumbled, *Starya doora*, Old fool, and leaving them to their loud disapproval, I ran.

Irina and another friend, Galka, were waiting for me in our usual spot. There was a lot to talk about, and it was all about Victor. Victor had only recently moved into the neighborhood to live with his grandparents. He was tall, pale, skinny, and utterly mysterious. He hardly spoke. He guarded his history with great care.

Victor had made no friends since he'd arrived, and with his stooped shoulders and sunken chest, he reminded me of a sickly tree. In short, he was fascinating.

The bravest among us had tried to get Victor to talk, but it didn't work, and the more closed he was, the more appealing he seemed. We conjectured endlessly about what he did after school and what he thought. Was his coldness the sad result of a broken heart? Did his silence hide the soul of a poet?

I had had no luck in breaking through the wall he'd built around himself, so I resorted to teasing. During geography class one day, our teacher asked if we could guess the height of Mt. Elbruce. Enthusiastically, we threw answers at Mrs. Olga Borisovna. All of them were wrong. Victor raised his hand, stood up, and gave the correct answer. Everyone, including our teacher, was amazed. I couldn't control myself.

"Maybe Victor knows because he's head and shoulders above all of us and can see better!" The class laughed. Victor's pale cheeks blazed deep red and his eyes flashed as he sat back down in his seat. For the rest of the class he kept his eyes trained on his desk. That seemed to finish off my chances with Victor.

A few days later it was growing even colder and I was still clinging to my thin sweater as I stood gossiping with Irina and Galka on our way home from school. The girl-chatter was winding down when we noticed Victor across the street, reading a poster tacked to a telephone pole. I realized I'd have to walk right by him on my way home. I said good-bye to Irina and Galka and crossed the road, followed by the sounds of their muffled giggling.

I didn't think Victor had seen me, but he turned and asked, "Can I walk you home?"

This was a question I had fantasized about, but certainly not one I expected to hear. Why would this unreachable stranger reach out to me all of a sudden? He took my heavy schoolbooks and we set off together. It was a short walk, but in no time I learned that Victor lived with his grandparents because his mother and her new husband had moved to another part of town and had no room for him, that his father had left when Victor was very young and nobody had heard from him in years, that his grandfather was ill and that Victor was worried. His stories made me silent. His life was very different from mine.

He was still talking when we got to my apartment block. I was surprised at how much he wanted to tell me about his life, when just an hour ago I had known nothing about him. I was freezing. I thought about the homework waiting for me and reached out to take back my bag of books. Victor would not let go.

The change in him was instant. Seeing my helplessness, he broke into a rare smile, revealing a jagged row of gray teeth. At first I tugged gently at the book bag, then harder and harder. I realized that this was no playful game. What I saw in his eyes was alarming. They had turned cold and mean. And now he gripped my fingers over the handle with his icy hands. I was suddenly frightened. The courtyard was empty and there were no passersby to help. Even the censura seemed to have abandoned their post.

My throat felt numb. But then a window above us flew open. A familiar voice yelled down: "Leave her alone, or I'll empty this pot of soup over your stupid head!" We both looked up. The winter-stocking watchdog had come to my rescue.

Victor let go and hissed, "I'll catch you later." He brushed past me, and with a quick stride of his lanky legs he was gone. The fourth-floor sentry didn't take her watchful eyes off him until he had disappeared from view. She leaned out of the window, looked to the left, looked to the right, assessed the situation in her territory, and satisfied that all was clear, drew back inside.

I never apologized to her for being rude about the stockings, and I never thanked her for saving me from Victor. But the next morning I passed by the row of Guardians and said a polite hello. The weather was much friendlier now that I was wearing my winter stockings.

THE HOSPITAL VISIT

SOMETHING STRANGE WAS HAPPENING TO BABUSHKA INNA'S BODY. WE WERE KNEADING DOUGH TOGETHER AT THE BLUE KITCHEN TABLE IN OUR APARTMENT. I ASKED HER WHY THE BASE OF HER NECK was swollen. "It is a *zob*," she said, "an inflammation of my glands. I will have to have it removed soon. You don't want your grandmother to look like a turkey, do you?"

I drew my flour-dipped finger along the swollen node.

"Will it hurt? How long will you be in hospital? Can I visit you there?"

She answered calmly. "It will take several weeks before I can come home, but to see your beautiful face from the window of my hospital room will make me heal faster."

I was frightened for her, but the thought of her coming back to our apartment to convalesce was exciting. Having Babushka Inna and her stories on hand all day was a prospect I relished.

Nobody who could help it checked into a Soviet hospital unprepared. Mama began laying the groundwork for Inna's surgery a week before she was due to enter hospital. The doctors and the nurses were overworked and underpaid, so it was hard for them to set priorities. Expensive gifts, flowers, and cards helped them to do so. We all still remembered the awful news about Papa's cousin. He had died in a hospital corridor waiting for his turn on a dialysis machine. No one was using it at the time, but it was on hold for a prominent Soviet official. I wondered if Papa's cousin, a dedicated communist, was comforted by this noble thought as he lay quietly dying.

Mama had done her work well, distributing the appropriate hand-outs to all the right doctors and nurses, and Babushka's surgery was a success. But Mama's work was not over.

Nobody actually expected to eat the scant and wretched food the hospital provided. Like most patients, Babushka would have to rely on her family to cook for her. Mama worked hard to make a soup that she could proudly pronounce "gentle enough" and mashed potatoes that were light and fluffy enough to be called "heavenly." Pouring the soup into a glass jar and filling white enamel bowls with mashed potatoes, then covering them with a plate, Mama wrapped it all in kitchen towels to keep it warm. The jars and bowls were placed in an old leather bag. The zipper was broken, but that didn't matter because it could not have been closed over all the food anyway.

Mama took the bag to the hospital and handed it, along with a few rubles, to a wide-hipped, tight-lipped nurse. She pocketed the money and took the bag, along with our loving get well wishes, up to the third floor where Babushka shared a room with five other women. Mama waited outside on the lawn, and eventually Babushka appeared at the window, waving her hand and acknowledging that the gentlest of soups and the most heavenly of potatoes had made their way to her.

Visiting the sick was a noble, but very difficult task, and not for the faint of heart. It required resilience, ingenuity, and bravery. It was common for sissies to leave the hospital in tears, having failed to make it over the hurdles between them and their loved ones.

The first hurdle was the matter of visiting hours. People couldn't just walk in. "Germs are everywhere," hospital officials often declared, and who knows how filthy we might have been. Visiting hours were posted on the wall, but they were ignored by hospital employees and visitors alike. You had to wait for an attendant who guarded the entry door. With an air of bureaucratic self-importance, the attendant, a woman in a dirty white coat, would offer each visitor a similar dirty coat, along with the palm of her hand, in expectation of the rubles necessary to be led to the right ward and the right bed.

It was not that these women wanted to be cruel or miserable. It was that they made a miserable salary. They had little choice but to take part in their secret guilds and the secret bribe culture. After all, they too had to survive. It wasn't only visitors who helped support these women. The sick paid them too, whenever they needed to be bathed or changed. Otherwise they would be left in the same blood-stained hospital gown for days until a nurse had time to change them and their oozing bandages. Inna loved being clean. Every clean gown cost her a ruble, and although it was a hardship for her, she paid the price.

Mama, quite sensibly, tried to talk me out of visiting Babushka Inna. "It is too far. She'll be home soon."

I was determined to see Inna. My friend Irina and I stood in three long lines for the two buses and the trolley that would take us to the hospital. When we finally got there, the hospital and its grounds were dazzling. Springtime and its generous brush had painted the park in which the hospital stood. The white brick building was surrounded by lovely cherry trees in full bloom. Patients in blue robes, accompanied by their families, walked like the actors in an old movie. Red tulips sprang from the brilliant green carpet of grass.

We paid little attention to the frayed, fading piece of paper nailed to a bulletin board that stated visiting hours. Instead, we waited at the front entrance by the guard's kiosk for an attendant to appear. The minutes passed. There was a man sitting in the kiosk, but he was not the attendant. No dirty-coated attendant was in sight.

Eventually, we asked the man in the kiosk when the attendant would be back. He looked around his newspaper at us. She had gone for lunch and might or might not return. What's more, he was also on a break and did not want to be disturbed. He slammed the small window of the kiosk shut.

Still hopeful, Irina and I positioned ourselves outside the window to wait for his break to be over. An hour passed. Through the window we watched him study the newspaper. "It is not his department," said a passerby.

This kind stranger told us to come back tomorrow, but the thought of traveling on two buses and a trolley again was not appealing.

Mama had told us that the far right third-storey window was Inna's room. Irina and I stood outside it on the lawn. The windows were wide open to the fresh breeze, letting in the sounds of the spring day. Irina and I thought that the breeze would carry our words too. We counted one, two, three. "Babushka, Babushka!"

Several elderly women heard us yelling and looked out the windows hopefully. None of them were Inna.

We weren't going to give up. We circled the building, looking for another entrance. We finally found the door where supplies were delivered. To our surprise, it was unattended. I went in first, while Irina stood outside to make sure no one saw us. When the coast was clear, she followed me. The hallway leading toward the stairs was empty, and on tiptoe we approached them. Above us we could hear the sound of hospital activities. We held our breath against the stench of cleaning liquid and the laughter that was bubbling up inside us. In just a moment or two, I'd be able to surprise Babushka Inna with a hug and the promise of a hot bath as soon as she came home to us.

As I took hold of the wooden railing and placed my foot on the first step, a large woman in a white hospital coat and a kerchief appeared at the end of the hall. She noticed us. Menacingly waving the mop she was holding, she charged at us like a prehistoric mammoth hunter about to make a kill.

Irina tugged my arm and we ran down the hall, out the door, and up the green hill. All the while the white-coated woman was swearing, "You little thieves, I'll get you! You little whores!"

The grandmothers who had looked at us out the windows earlier appeared at the windows again. We were a welcome diversion from blood and urine tests. Babushka Inna was not among them, and I was grateful. When the woman finally ran out of steam and turned to go back into the building, I said to Irina, "You look like a beet."

"So do you."

We returned home defeated. The long bus ride drained the color that we'd acquired from the mop-lady. We were weak from hunger and disappointment. Mindless bureaucracy, one point. Compassion, zero.

Inna came home a week later. With a white patch under her chin, she moved around the apartment gingerly, taking delight in every clean corner and at everything we did for her. Mama laid out fresh towels and a robe, while Natasha and I drew warm water in our deep, white tub. We helped her undress, trying not to notice her naked body or to touch her incision. Her body smelled of the hospital, an odor she was anxious to wash away. She looked vulnerable, but unashamed, as she let us help her into the tub. As the water parted to receive her body she gave a soft sigh of joy.

No one spoke as Natasha and I soaped her back. I knew that Natasha must be thinking of all her bonds with Inna: their love of the summer that would come soon, slow country walks, verses of poetry they exchanged, and music they both loved, especially the opening movement of Tchaikovsky's first piano concerto that always made them cry. I was not jealous of their secrets, because Inna and I shared secrets of our own.

My great-grandmother, Inna's mother, was called Liza. She lived in a tiny shtetl in the Ukrainian countryside. The family had a small store where you could buy everything from a loaf of bread to a box of nails. Liza had a small, frail brother named Yossele. Yossele had been sickly all his life and required a lot of care. He adored his older sister, Liza, and followed her everywhere. When the time came for him to go to *cheder*, Jewish school, where he would learn to read and write Hebrew, as well as learn stories from the Bible and Jewish history, a problem presented itself. Yossele refused to go without Liza.

This was unheard of. Girls were educated at the stove by their mothers. But Yossele could not be budged. The *melamed*, the teacher, was called for consultation. He was served a glass of tea and day-old *rugelach* left over from the store, thoughtfully warmed for such an honored guest.

Hearing the problem and seeing the pale Yossele peeking from behind the stove, the teacher assessed the situation. The boy looked sickly and weak and probably would not live long. "It is a *mitzvah*, a good deed, to learn. What harm can it do? If your daughter wants to accompany him, I will allow it. She will sit and wait for him while he learns." Without a glance at Liza he left the house.

On the first day of school, Yossele and Liza appeared in the schoolhouse. She wore a white kerchief over her dark, wavy hair, and patched woolen stockings covered her legs. She was the only girl in the room. This didn't bother Yossele, who would not let go of her hand as Liza sat right next to him on a wooden bench, but the other boys began to snicker.

With his bearded chin waggling, the melamed motioned to Liza to sit in the back of the room where Yossele could comfort himself with a reassuring glance at her every now and then, but where she would not be a distraction.

"For all those long hours, I did needlepoint, but I could not help but hearing the lessons and learning," she told her daughter, Ginda, the girl who would one day shed her Jewish name and become Inna. "Sitting on that back bench, I heard, I learned, I remembered."

I watched the suds and water run down Inna's limbs, forming circles all around her, just as it had formed circles when I was small, and she was the one bathing me.

I remembered playing in the water while she told me an ancient story about the Exodus and the Jewish slaves who fled from Egypt, and for whom God parted the Sea of Reeds to make them free. Using my hands, I tried to part the waters of my bath.

"How can it be?" I said. "You can't part water!"

Nobody was supposed to be religious under the Soviets and Inna was not a religious person. But somehow, talk of God came easily to her. Along with the name, Ginda, her mother had blessed her with the marvelous quality of being able to see a bit of magic in life despite its everyday dreariness. She explained the parting of the water to me with a sense of wonder.

"It was a miracle. Only God can do it." And she would tell me other stories, about the brave King David who killed Goliath, and wise King Solomon, who judged two women. Her stories made me forget that my eyes were stinging from cheap Soviet shampoo. They were the stories she had learned from her mother who sat on the back bench so many years ago. Now they were my treasures, tiny sparkling diamonds that brightened the drab Soviet gray. Though Ginda had vanished along with the shtetl, to be survived by the sophisticated, no-longer religious Inna, she remembered what she had learned. By the time her stories reached me, there were no more cheders and no more melameds. Stalin had seen to it. The power of the stories remained, but I told no one what I had learned. Judaism had no place in Soviet life.

I held the large bar of soap in one hand while I washed her back carefully, feeling the snowy white skin, smooth and warm and alive under my hand. Natasha and I dried Babushka Inna with Mama's clean towels. We wrapped her in her comfortable robe as she whispered, "*Spasibo* – Thank you," to us. As if she had read my thoughts, she said, "I remember when I bathed you two. Thank God I have lived long enough to see my granddaughters bathe me."

Inna's voice was soft, but triumphant.

THE UNKNOWN SOLDIER

As always, the school principal was dressed in a suit. Before she put out her hand to stop me as I passed her in the hallway, I had time to notice that it was a green knit that clung to her tall, shapely figure like an autumn glove.

"Traitor!" Boiling and seething like one of Mama's pots on the stove, she towered over me with red, fiery hair and flushed cheeks. "You little traitor! This country gave you everything. Education, medical care, jobs for your parents. And after all of this, you want to leave your motherland for another country?"

The small group of students encircling us was beginning to turn into a crowd, as the principal's voice grew louder. Sensing a teaching opportunity for anyone who might dare to follow in my treacherous footsteps, the principal raised her voice even more.

"The Soviet people sacrificed their lives and fought so you could live in peace. And this is how you repay that sacrifice? Grimberg, from this moment you may never again come to school. We remove you from all activities associated with our school and our students!"

Curtly, she handed me my record folder, turned sharply, and marched down the hall. With that I was officially an outcast. The crowd of students stared at me. My cheeks burned and tears stung my eyes as if someone had slapped me. I stared at the school's uneven linoleum floor. There was nowhere to hide. When I dared to look up, I saw the faces of pupils from my own class, girls I had known all my life. Their expressions ranged from compassion to pure resentment and indignation. Just moments earlier we had been friends, chatting about our summer and the upcoming fall schedule. Now a great chasm had opened up between us. My life now had a before and after. I ran down the corridor and two flights of stairs alone. Nobody spoke to me. Nobody wanted to be seen near the traitor.

When I came out, blinking into the sunshine of the schoolyard, Papa was waiting for me. Despite my protests, he had insisted on coming with me to school and he insisted on waiting for me outside, while I gathered up my belongings and records.

Papa looked like someone I hardly knew as he stood patiently against the cement wall of the schoolyard. Until that moment I had never thought of him as a short man, but now I was struck by his size, his graying temples, and his slight figure. I buried my face in his chest and inhaled the familiar odor of cigarettes, sweet aftershave, and sadness. The early autumn sun warmed us generously as we walked home. On that September morning, Mother Nature seemed more forgiving and less jealous than our motherland.

In the mid-1970s, the whole Soviet Union was facing a hungry time because the wheat crop had failed. In order to feed its population, the Russian government was forced to approach North

America in order to buy grain. The purchase was accomplished, but not before the Soviet Union was pressured to loosen its hold on certain "oppressed" minorities by allowing them to leave. *Oppressed* was interpreted by the Soviets to mean "undesirable," and "undesirable" included Jews. A window of opportunity had opened to us, but no one knew for how long.

With the announcement of the wheat exchange, the idea of departure – the virus – had entered our home. Once we were infected with it, we had to make a decision that we knew could not be reversed and would change our lives forever. At first, Mama and Papa's urgent, whispered conversations would end abruptly when Natasha or I entered the room. They tried to protect us from worry, and they didn't want to give us information that someone could use against us. The tension finally broke when we gathered around our small, blue kitchen table. Papa's usual dreamy demeanor gave way to a no-nonsense practicality. It seemed a new spirit had entered him. Firmly and resolutely, he laid out all the good that could come from leaving, and all the difficulties that might lie ahead. Finally, he asked us to vote. I was only fifteen, but my vote counted too. If any of us decided that we could not leave our home, our relatives, and friends, then we would all stay without placing guilt or blame anywhere.

The time had come to decide, because it would take almost a year between making an application for departure and actually getting the permission to depart. It would be a year of exile, living in our own home. We would not be able to work or go to school while we waited for the unpredictable Soviet authorities to grant us exit visas.

I looked into my teacup in search of an answer. If I voted to stay, we would continue to share our lives with the aunts, uncles, and cousins that I loved. I would never have to leave my shining knights – the three stately chestnut trees that guarded our building – or the rolling green hills of the countryside outside Kiev, where ancient oaks extended their broad branches. I would not have to leave behind the language I spoke or the culture that was mine. Of course, I could always speak Russian to my family, but the new place we would call home would be different. I would have to live surrounded by language and customs that were utterly foreign to me.

Then there were the good things that might come with the decision to leave: Mama and I would never have to stand frozen in food lines again. I would be able to own a dress that my sister didn't hand down to me. I could study at a university where it wouldn't matter that I was a Jew. And I would be able to travel.

I don't remember how long we sat with our cups of cooling tea, hesitating to look at one another, but eventually Natasha and I spoke up together. We wanted to leave, even though it meant going into the unknown. Mama's hand shook slightly as she wiped her tears. She knew the losses and pain in store for us either way. And she knew what loss was like. Our cousin Vitaly, her sister's son, had drowned under mysterious circumstances at university although he was a master swimmer. There was no measure of Mama's guilt and sadness over leaving her grieving sister, but Natasha and I had to come first. "If the girls desire to go, then I will go too."

Now I was branded a traitor. Though I missed school and the classmates who'd been my friends, I wasn't bored during the long months between our announcement and our receiving permission to leave. I was surrounded by other teenagers whose families had also made the decision to venture into the great unknown. All of us were living in twilight, cut off from everything: school, sports, and work. We spent hours together, walking streets that seemed unfamiliar during school hours, and gathering in each others' homes to talk and plan. Our lives hung, suspended in the air like an unfinished bridge across a river.

Of all the things that were now forbidden to me, there was only one that I ached for. Grades 9 and 10 of our school had the honor of standing on guard at the Grave of the Unknown Soldier, and I longed to take my place among them to celebrate Kiev's Soviet victory over the Nazis.

Fierce battles raged between the Russians and the Nazis for Kiev in 1942, and thousands of young men lost their lives defending the ancient Russian capital. Like autumn leaves, they were scattered across the fields, waiting for burial.

Victory finally came after four unbearable, unspeakable years of war, and it was celebrated with great joy. May 9 was declared a holiday marked by military parades, stirring speeches, and songs. By then spring was on its way, and Kiev was at its most beautiful, blanketed in tulips, lilacs, and chestnut blossoms that fell from the trees like soft, pink rain.

Natasha celebrates May 9 with her friends.

The victory parade was held in the center of Kiev with special bleachers set aside for Soviet officials. The grand marches were a promise that our military might would never again allow our country to be invaded. Widows would take their husbands' medals out of the safety of velvet boxes, polish them with great care, and pin them to their dresses as they prepared to march proudly on behalf of the fallen. Elderly people, decorated with war honors, waved flowers and glowed with pride. Afterwards, people danced in the streets, mostly women with women. The war had taken away their men.

The effects of the war on Russia and its culture lasted for generations. Songs, movies, and poetry spoke of losses and courage, death and victory. Young and old, we all knew these songs. My sister and I could join in effortlessly when our parents and their friends sang or recited famous war poems by heart. The poet Racul Gamzatov wrote lyrics to a song that made me cry every time I heard it. "Cranes" describes how, in a low, soft voice, one seasoned soldier, a survivor of war, sings to his comrades who did not return.

The soldier describes a flock of cranes soaring above him. In mournful tones, they seem to be calling someone's name, and the soldier notices they have left a space in their formation. "Perhaps they are keeping it for me," the soldier says. One day he, too, will join the flock. "And you, who here on earth remain, will hear my loud and strident cry."

Many of the fallen were never found. Many more could not be identified because of terrible injuries that had made them unrecognizable. They were put to rest in a communal grave that became known as the Grave of the Unknown Soldier, marked by a stately monument. The monument, a tall granite obelisk, rose above Kiev's green landscape. An eternal flame burned at its base. The soldiers' names were etched on the black granite walls in alphabetical order, too many to read or even to count. The foot of the monument was seldom visible. Usually it was buried under bouquets of flowers brought there by newlyweds and those who wanted to mark their gratitude for the soldiers' sacrifice.

In a state where there was supposed to be no religion, this was the closest thing to a shrine or sanctuary we knew. The sight of the monument demanded thoughtfulness and respect. On either side of it, in rain, snow, and summer heat, students dressed in white and army gray, marched solemnly or stood motionless in total silence, guarding the eternal flame. They looked stoic and strong.

For years, I had dreamed of being old enough to take my turn standing guard. To stand on guard was a personal honor. Each of us had been touched by the war. Very few of us had grandfathers. We were raised by grandmothers whose husbands left and never returned from the battlefields. The

Inna and David. My father's father went to war, but died of his wounds not long after he returned.

Inna begged David to take her with him but he did not. She had his children to raise.

Russian people's losses were impossible to comprehend. There was not a family that had not lost someone: a father, brother, or son – and sometimes all of them. Standing on guard by the monument let us show respect and gratitude. It was the way to demonstrate to our families and the nation how much their sacrifice meant to us.

It would have been a way for me to bear witness that my father's father, David Solomonovitch Grimberg, went to war and served four years in the infantry division of the Red Army. He was wounded twice. He was lucky enough to live to see the Soviet victory over the Nazis, and to embrace my grandmother and his two sons upon his return. Cruelly, he died of his wounds not long after the war ended.

For my grandmother, Inna, May 9 was bittersweet. "What a pity David did not live to see his sons grow up. He left us so young," she would say. For a while after he died, he would visit her from time to time in her dreams, sometimes looking sick, and sometimes handsome and healthy. She begged him to take her with him. Life was unbearable without him. But he would not. She had his children to raise.

Eventually, he left even her dreams and she was truly alone. All that remained of his image and his spirit were what Inna captured and preserved in the stories she told us. I knew the stories by heart, yet I begged to hear them over and over again. As each year passed, they seemed more majestic and noble to me. While Grandmother Inna worked at the kitchen table, I asked her the same questions about the same people and the same events. My questions never seemed tiresome to her. She always responded with a sad pleasure in her voice. Every story began with the familiar opening: "It was before the war," or "It was after the war." For her, life was divided in two. Whether an event took place a decade before the war or decades after, it did not matter. The tragedy that had befallen the country, and every person in it, drew a stark, divisive line through her life. These stories were so much a part of me that when her words stopped as her fingers left the dough she was kneading to reach for another ingredient, I could continue for her.

Dedushka David was one of eleven children. The son of a wealthy Kiev merchant, he grew up in a loud, busy household. With the outbreak of the Communist Revolution, the family wealth was confiscated. To survive Soviet purges, he erased the link to his wealthy family by changing his last name. All that was left of his privileged upbringing was a generous spirit, love of beauty, irresistible charm, and memories: of a flour mill near their spacious house in the heart of Kiev, scraps of French – learned from a governess – and long seders in the large dining room.

David met my grandmother, Inna, the only surviving child of doting parents, when she was just eighteen. Her quick mind and superb memory had been honed by the two sad noblewomen who had taught her so well. People who met her didn't know that her alabaster skin and shining black braids, full sensuous lips and wide brown eyes hid a quick temper and steely willfulness.

When David and Inna first married, things were not always smooth. My grandfather had chosen a beautiful, clever bride who was used to having her own way. Grandfather worked long hours. As soon as he came home, Inna served him a plate of food on a three-legged table that was pushed into the corner in order to keep it upright. Grandfather sat on an old wooden chair, and after the first hellos, he would pick up his newspaper and lose himself in its pages.

This retreat infuriated Inna. After all, she had been working all day and wanted the company of her husband. Often she took stock of a room that was furnished with the barest necessities: a few wooden chairs, a bed with a sunken, fish-belly mattress, a three-legged table, and a husband barricaded behind a newspaper wall. And each time she rebelled in the same way. She would slam out the door and run to the neighbors.

It always worked. Grandfather patiently folded his newspaper and went next door to fetch her home. He would pull the shaky chair from the table, and draw her onto his lap. "Ginda, I breathe the air without noticing, but I can't live without it. That's how I feel about you. You think I don't notice you, but I can't live without you." And so the fight would end tenderly. They adored each other.

In 1940, a white draft notice appeared in the mailbox. Every able-bodied Soviet man was needed to fight the Nazis. Inna found the notice and she cried. When the time came for him to leave, she hugged my papa, Zimochka, and my Uncle Valya and told them to say good-bye to their father. She wanted to walk her husband to the train station alone. They took a familiar path that led by the river. They noticed nothing but the

My father's parents adored each other.

willow trees that, as if in anticipation of the grief to come, lowered their branches into the water.

Letters followed. A handful of them survive, stored carefully with the other family heirlooms in the top drawer of my parents' dining room cabinet. In 1943, when Papa was only twelve, his father was wounded. He wrote to Papa from the hospital in a steady, clear hand:

My beloved, my dearest Zimochka!
I received all your letters. They brought me joy. Remember, Zimochka, when I left for war, you did not write very well yet, and now you write like an adult. My wounds are healing, though I still walk with a cane. I can't leave the hospital yet and feel very bored, so I read a lot. Local school children come to sing and dance for us. Sometimes they show us a movie.

Zimochka, when I was wounded and they carried me from the battlefield, I was placed in a little sled that was pulled to the medical station by five dogs. The dogs are an incredible help to us during battles. Some of them carry bullets and ammunition when the fighting is at its worst. They can make it into the most dangerous and narrowest of places. Attached to their backs are belts with pockets filled with bandages and medicine.

When I return, I will tell you many more interesting things. Zimochka, study hard and well. Help Mama, Babushka and Dedushka, and do not tease Valushka. Live well together. Now is a difficult time and food is scarce, so don't be picky, and eat all you are offered.

I love and kiss you dearly.

Your papa, David

My uncle Valya was playing in the street outside the apartment building on a beautiful day in May, 1945. As he ran past the gate he noticed a man in uniform slouched on the steps, resting his head on the railing. So it fell to the boy to carry the great news. "Mama, Mama, Papa is back. Come home quickly!" he yelled. Inna could never find the words to describe her joy. Her beloved David had come home.

He was tired and ill from the pain of his wounds. Papa and my uncle Valya were thrilled and shy in front of the man in uniform who was their father. They approached him cautiously at first. The man wanted to know about their school, the books they were reading, and their friends. He could tell that the boys were different one from the other and asked them how they got along together, for he suspected that they often fought. "Are you good to one another?" he asked.

Papa whispered, "Valya calls me names."

"What kind of names does he call you?"

"*Shgeed*. Kike. The kids in school call me kike too."

Valya defended himself. "A kid at school called me a dirty shgeed so when Zimka makes me mad, that's what I call him."

"I don't like it," said Papa. "Tell him to stop."

The trace of a smile crossed Grandfather's face. "Valushka, you cannot call Zimka a shgeed, because you are a Jew. When people hate Jews they call them these names. Your friends probably don't mean it, but this they hear from adults."

Fascinated with his badges and buttons, the boys drew closer. They examined their father's khaki uniform, the worn leather belt, the few medals proudly displayed. Papa was impressed. "Tell us about the war. Were you scared?"

Inna had made David a drink of warm milk and honey. He sipped it before he answered. "Zimochka, it is hard to be brave in a battle. It is chaos. Bullets fly so close that they scratch your cheeks, and your comrades die by your side. But because you are a Jew, you cannot hide behind other soldiers. You must be one of the first in battle. The eyes of the world are always upon a Jew." Papa never forgot those words.

Grandfather served the entire four years of war in the infantry. His wounds never healed. When he died, he left Inna and his small sons, along with millions of other widows and orphans, in a country ravaged by hunger and poverty.

The date when our class was to guard the monument had been set long before I was expelled. Though I knew I would not be allowed to take part, I could simply not stay away. As I approached the monument where my classmates were gathering, the rain began to fall. The day was gray and somber. Most of the birds that made their summer home in the woods nearby had flown south. In a few weeks the rest would follow.

I watched my classmates enviously as they stood, solemn and proud, at the monument. Their eyes shone and their cheeks and noses were red from the cold. They had learned how to march, turn; and stand. Toes pointing, arms swinging to and fro in a silent, uniform rhythm, they marched and stood in silence until it was time to change guards. Their dignity made my heart ache to be one of them.

When they were finished I went along with them to an old school nearby, where the honor guard could warm up and change. Woolen jackets and boots were spread out on the heaters to dry. The humid little room smelled of wet wool and sweat.

I listened to the familiar voices as they made fun of the teachers and complained companionably about homework. They talked about how proud they were to have stood and marched so perfectly. I tried my best to join in, and they were kind to me. But our life paths now seemed to run parallel to each other and would never cross again. They avoided asking me questions. After a few moments, I said good-bye and slipped away. I was already an expatriate.

As I headed toward the bus, I passed by the Grave of the Unknown Soldier once again. Its flame seemed even brighter in the gray autumn dusk. With a heavy heart, I took a deep breath. I recited the words, "Like autumn leaves, bodies of soldiers were scattered all over these fields. Touched by death, their eyes wide open as if surprised, they looked up into the sky. . . ."

In my jumble of thoughts I remembered the principal's poisonous green suit and her words. "You traitor . . . sacrifice . . . for you." I don't remember how long I stood looking at the flame, but what made me look up was the sound coming from high above me. The silence was interrupted by a series of strong guttural bird cries. With their long necks extended and their legs stretched, white cranes soared in a beautiful V formation above the monument. Feeling chilled, I exhaled and headed home.

I DREAM OF FLORENCE

On a late-summer afternoon, not long before the chance came for us to leave the Soviet Union, I was standing in line at the library, waiting to check out a tottering pile of novels. As I shifted my weight from foot to foot, I noticed a large, colorful volume of photos entitled *Florence* lying on one of the wooden reading tables. Though the wait had been long and it was almost my turn, I stepped out of the line and slipped into a chair to look at the book. As I turned the glossy pages, the draughty, poorly lit reading room in which I sat seemed to fade away. I was in Florence.

Our two rooms and miniature kitchen didn't offer many places for quiet thinking, so almost from the time I could read, at nightfall I threw my coat over my shoulders, made my way to the library, and took my place at a table near the window that looked out onto our street. I barricaded myself with books. When I found an irresistible quote or poem, I would copy it into my battered diary. The diary bulged with pictures of beautiful men and women I'd cut out of magazines and pasted on the pages. In and around the pictures and poems, I wrote down my private thoughts and feelings, using cryptic words or sentence fragments so that they would remain safely mine.

I loved copying beautiful words by hand into my gray diary, especially in the winter, when the soft snow fell gently outside the window and muted the sound of children laughing as they rode home on sleds pulled by their parents.

The library's collection was very poor. The best of the books had been stolen or sent on to the central branch. Even when I was lucky enough to find a good book on the shelves, the most interesting pages were often missing, cut out by a fine razor or simply torn away. It was strange. The person using the razor obviously loved the words on those pages but with a love that had turned destructive and possessive. At times I felt that Razorhand and I were secretly bound by the love we shared for written words. But he was faster than I, and got to the pages first.

Sometimes, in my dreams, I would meet Razorhand Wordlover between the bookshelves. I'd make him fall in love with me, and once he was smitten, I would force him to swear he'd never mar a book again. He would take me to the place where he kept all those lovely verses and offer them to me – like a precious gift.

That's why the beautiful illustrated book about Florence was such a wonderful surprise. Against all odds, it was still intact.

I shivered as I turned the pages in the hot, still air. I was looking at something that was forbidden to me. Good Soviet citizens had no need to leave the motherland. It was disloyal to crave travel, but I couldn't help it. I was drawn into each of the colored photographs of Florence, the narrow cobblestone streets that led me to a gorgeous fountain splashing in a square, the carefree people sitting under bright umbrellas happily sipping their coffee. I drank in the sight of exquisite churches, the glorious white marble statues, the painted ceilings covered in images of heaven and hell.

I don't remember how much time I spent looking at that book, but when I closed the covers I pushed it away from me abruptly, as if it were burning my hands. I sat for a long time and when I got up, a strange feeling I could not name hung over me.

That night I dreamed of Florence. I walked its narrow streets and pulled open the heavy wooden doors of its Renaissance churches. I wrapped a bright silk scarf around my shoulders and strained my neck as I looked up at the images floating on the ceiling of the Duomo. I sipped bitter coffee at an outdoor café and smiled at the men in their long white aprons and bow ties. I ate pizzetta and scooped up a string of the soft cheese that collected on my chin.

The next morning as I sat across from Natasha, picking at Mama's breakfast omelet, I announced, "I would love to see Florence. Wouldn't you?"

Natasha stared back at me, her brown eyes full of bitter laughter. Those eyes said it all. *Are you out of your mind? You will never see Florence, or anywhere else outside the Soviet Union. The authorities would never allow it.*

I knew what she was thinking and I knew she was right. The only people to be issued visas and passports were the select few who traveled "outside" under the watchful eyes of Soviet activists or informers.

Now with the window open in 1978, our chance for travel had come. As it had in our family, the idea spread like a virus throughout Kiev, and in urgent whispered conversations, Jews shared what information they had.

My parents' friends gathered in one another's homes and spoke in low, secretive voices, comparing the nuggets of information they had gleaned about the New World. Even those who had friends or relatives in the West had very limited, censored news. Most of what we knew about the world beyond the Iron Curtain came through rumors and letters festooned with the censors' black ink scribbles. A fact of daily life was that our letters were routinely opened and read by unknown readers. These censors became participants in our lives. They were the first to learn of the triumphs and defeats of our loved ones in the New World. They knew before we did that a cousin had had a baby, or that an uncle had found a new job. They were the ones who decided what we could know and what should be stricken out with lines of thick black ink that bled through the page and made the other side of the letter hard to read. Many things made in the Soviet Union were of poor quality. However, the black ink that blotted out the words of the people we loved did its job admirably. I often thought that it would have been kinder to destroy the letters altogether, but the black ink was there to remind us and everyone else who saw it, that a harsh Soviet eye and a heavy Soviet hand played a major role in our lives.

Those unknown readers weren't the only ones who kept track of us. We knew that people listened to every phone conversation, so we spoke in code to one another. Unidentified agents were everywhere. We could feel it.

The Soviets made the decision to leave as difficult as they could. Sometimes they granted exit visas to elderly parents but not to their children, sending out of the country the most vulnerable without the protection of their family. They deliberately granted visas in a way that would rend families apart. All of us knew of painful situations where one married child was prepared to leave but the other was not. That meant that the parents had to choose which child to give up. Whatever the decision, it would split their family for years or, more likely, forever. Inna had to make that decision. She would come with us, leaving Uncle Valya and his family behind.

Rumors circulated that the window of departure could be closed at any time, and the chance to exit the Soviet Union would be lost if we didn't act right away. We'd be stranded, branded as traitors, no longer at home in our own home. Papa hurried to apply for us to leave. We waited and waited for the permission to come. Every day I was sent to the mailbox to see if the small white envelope was there. Eight tense months had passed by the time a stranger showed up at our door.

"Is your papa home?"

I showed him into the apartment. The man's face was very pale and his eyes were watery blue. He anxiously crushed and twisted his cap in his red, chapped hands. "I have special information for you regarding your status," he said to Papa. "I am a member of the Soviet militia, and I have been informed that your exit visas have been issued. You should receive them any time now."

Before his words could sink in, he cleared his throat. "My new wife and I will be given your apartment when you leave." He had brought the news in person so that he could see our apartment, because it would be his new home. The housing shortage affected the Soviet police, just like everyone else, and they waited along with the rest of us, in the dark and in the light, for the opportunity to improve their lives.

Mama was not home, so to mark the momentous news, Papa sent me to the store to buy herring, pickles, and two onions. We already had a bottle of *Stolichnaya*, Russian vodka, in the cupboard. When I got back, Papa transferred the smoked herring from a greasy newspaper wrapper onto a white plate, coarsely sliced the onions and spread them on the herring, and then poured oil over both. I was impressed. I'd never seen Papa prepare food of any kind before. It was a job he left to Mama.

The two men filled their small vodka glasses and raised them. "To you," said Papa. He looked around at our kitchen walls. "*Snovoselym*," which means something like, "To your new home."

"To you," said the stranger, following Papa's gaze. "*Horoshey dorogy!* Bon Voyage!"

In one gulp they emptied their glasses, slammed them down, and proclaimed in unison, "Aaaah!" They plunged their forks into the plate of herring and onions and filled their glasses once more.

I stood in the entryway to the kitchen, watching the men as they toasted each other again and again. Papa's refined manners and the stranger's rough ones were an oddly riveting combination. It wouldn't have occurred to either of them to spend an evening drinking together under any other circumstances. But the more they drank and the more loudly they toasted, the less distance there was between them. For a couple of hours in Mama's absence, the welcome informer and my gentlemanly Papa sat at our kitchen table drinking and toasting, first to the Soviet militia man's move, and then to our move.

After the man left, Papa, supported by the kitchen cabinet, looked, to say the least, relaxed. He was always affectionate toward Mama, but that night he was especially so, when she got home and he announced to her that our visas were about to arrive. We were on our way.

Even though my parents and so many others spent their lives scrimping so that they could put a portion of their meager salaries aside, Soviet officials did not allow anyone to remove their savings in either money, or in valuables from the country. If we wanted to go, it would mean starting new lives without a penny.

We were permitted to take very few belongings with us. We learned that we could keep our books, but only if they had been published after 1960 and thus, were not considered valuable. Most of our favorites had to be left behind. Handwritten and typed papers were also suspect, and would have to be destroyed or left behind. I held on to my diary for as long as I could, but two nights before we were to leave, I closed the kitchen door and lit a match to it. I watched as a small flame consumed the words I loved so much and turned them into ash. The magazine pictures of beautiful people put up a little struggle, but they too gave in, and in the end, they were washed down the drain with icy water.

We sold almost everything else we had or gave it away. We gave the cold cellar, a priceless gift, to our neighbor Olga, who volunteered to keep our beloved (by Mama, at least), impossibly moody cat, Shusha.

We gave away the blue kitchen table where Bronya and then Inna had baked for us over the years, where I wrote my first compositions with Mama, and where we made our decision to leave Kiev. After that we ate, army-style, over the wooden boxes that held the belongings we were leaving behind. At the end, we slept on mattresses on the floor. I found this exciting, but it terrified Mama.

We'd received a letter from friends abroad, in which the Secret Hand of the censors neglected to erase the news that, for some reason, Italian men seemed to enjoy buying painted wooden *Matrushkas* (stacking dolls), Ukrainian spoons, and bowls as gifts for their wives. This was an important scrap of advice and we followed it, as did many others who were preparing to leave. First our apartment, and then our suitcases began to fill up with Russian and Ukrainian souvenirs. Matrushkas, brightly colored wooden spoons and bowls, embroidered cotton towels, and mini samovars, trinkets we would never before have dreamed of keeping in our home, were crammed into our suitcases so that we would have something we could sell or give along the way in return for any kindness shown to us by strangers.

We left Kiev on a warm spring day. The Soviet bureaucrats (not the media, because our leaving was not publicized) involved with granting our papers had all said "You will cry for your homeland forever. We will never let you come back." The tears began to flow that day.

The Old Guard was firmly ensconced on the benches. It seemed that almost everyone else in the building had spilled into the courtyard, or watched us through their open windows, as we kissed and embraced the friends who came to say good-bye.

Not all our friends. Only those who were brave enough to do so. We longed for one last chance to see the people we had cared about all our lives, and we knew that our good-byes were final ones. The curtain would close behind us. But the Soviet officials had branded us as traitors, and anyone seen with us was

Some of the good friends we left behind. Our good-byes were final ones.

in danger of being called a traitor by association. We understood, but we were heartsick, about those who stayed away.

According to the Soviets, we deserved to be punished, and the penalty was never being allowed to return to the place of our birth or to the people we left. And punished we were, in ways more painful than they could ever know. Inna's tears as she hugged my Uncle Valya good-bye were bitter evidence of their cruelty.

We piled our flimsy red cardboard suitcases and our huge duffel bags into a friend's car for the ride to the train station. As we drove away I whispered farewell to my chestnut trees, the three shining knights of my past life. They were full of blossoms, aromatic and sweet. I did not promise them I would return, because I knew I never would.

When we arrived at the train station in Kiev, we were met by the most courageous of our friends, those who dared to be seen in a public place with traitors to the state. We wept as we kissed them for the last time.

We traveled all day and well into the evening to the western border of Ukraine and the town of Chop. We passed a sleepless night in the limbo of a freezing cold hotel, waiting silently for morning to come. The next day we would go through a final inspection of our belongings and our documents at the train station. Once we had our exit visas and the proper documents, we would be allowed to board the train that would take us through the vivid green Carpathian Mountains beyond Chop, through what was then Czechoslovakia, and on to Vienna. Austria was the West.

In Vienna the Hebrew Immigrant Aid Society (HIAS) would help us. Those people who had chosen to go to Israel would be flown out of Vienna right away. Those of us who were going on to the United States, Canada, or Australia would be sent to Italy to wait there for entry visas to our final destinations.

It was the first of May and Chop sported its May Day decorations, Soviet flags and banners, proclaiming glory to Soviet achievements and successes. How strange we must have looked, walking through the town, back to the train station on our way to the West. Carrying our four red cardboard suitcases stuffed with souvenirs and the heavy duffle bags, we made our way through the crowded ancient streets, first Papa, then Mama, then Inna, and Natasha and me.

We passed marchers carrying red banners emblazoned with slogans: "Glory to our Soviet life and its communist future. Lenin's words live forever and ever!" They glared at us. The words *Traitors, traitors* were written on their faces.

There was something so tragically funny about the scene that I wanted to laugh. A couple of years before I had been a May Day marcher too, but even then, I was out of step.

On the first of May, parades were held all over the Soviet Union and our school held an elaborate one of its own. So that we'd move in unison, making impressive-looking formations, our gym teacher lined us up according to height, from the tallest to the shortest. I was almost the shortest person in the class, and I was placed in what would be the closing row next to another student named Ilana.

Ilana was a midget. At first she had to put up with curious stares and giggles, but by now we were used to her unusual stature. Ilana could hold her own anywhere. Her dark, shining ponytail was tied on top of her head to give her additional height. It was always gathered in a gauzy white bow. The bow was matched by her impeccable white stockings. She wore shiny patent leather shoes. It was obvious that someone at home loved

Ilana and took good care of her. There was a dignity and pride about her that made her stand tall.

The closing line was important, because it was the last impression people would have of our class's marching unit. So that we would be a worthy closing row, Ilana and I spent hours practicing our stride behind the school building. We pointed our toes, stretched our necks, and swung our arms from side to side, doing our best to resemble the soldiers who guarded Lenin's mausoleum. And just like the Soviet army, we were issued khaki uniforms. We wore jaunty soldiers' caps, decorated with a red star, tilted on the sides of our heads.

On May Day, stony-faced Soviet officials took their places with the school principal on wooden bleachers that had been newly built around the track in the playing field especially for the occasion. They offered lengthy formal greetings and finally settled in to judge the marchers.

The band began to play and we took our places. Our class stepped precisely to the music, and Ilana and I, heads held high, marched proudly in the closing row. At first, all went well. We smiled brightly at the judges. We marched with our toes pointed and we swung our short arms as hard as we could so that we would look like invincible Soviet soldiers. We had practiced, but we weren't prepared for what happened next. The rows ahead of us picked up speed and began to move faster. Ilana and I could not match their stride. To bridge the gap we stepped faster and faster. It didn't help. We were falling behind. The gap between us and the rest of the class grew wider. We forgot about pointed toes and precise swinging arms, and we began to run. Our beautiful caps slid down our faces, but we didn't give up. We pounded after the others. Natasha was sitting in the stands with her friends. They were shrieking and wiping their eyes. Even the marble-faced Soviet officials laughed.

As the rest of the class came to a neat halt, Ilana and I finally caught up to them. Humiliated, red-faced, and out of breath, we fell to the grass at the end of the field. Natasha clambered down from the bleachers and ran to us, her eyes full of concern, but her mouth shut tight to hold in her laughter.

I prayed for the coarse blades of grass to cover me.

I wondered if Ilana would risk taking part in this year's May Day march, the march that was supposed to affirm the achievements and progress of the Soviet nation. Knowing her gumption, I imagined she would. I was taking a risk too, marching in an altogether different direction, away from the Soviet Union and all its glory.

As soon as we got to the train station I disappeared into a filthy washroom that smelled of burning urine and chlorine. Hiding in a stall, I fastened a thin necklace around my neck. It belonged to my mother's friend, Polina. It wasn't worth much to anyone else, but it was an heirloom that had been handed from mother to daughter in Polina's family. She had wept when she gave it to Mama for safekeeping because her family was larger than ours and were at the limit of what they were allowed to take out of the country. We were determined to keep the necklace safe for Polina and return it to her when we all reached the West. The chain was long on me. It reached almost to my waist. Someone would have had to unbutton my shirt completely to see it.

It was a stupid and dangerous thing to do. If I got caught, we all could have been delayed and our exit visas canceled. We'd be left like fish, stranded on the shore, with no home ahead or behind us. We'd heard that there were random searches of the women and that modest pieces of jewelry, that meant nothing to anyone else, were stripped from their necks or wrists.

At the train station an area had been closed off for the final inspection, with one gate we passed through from the station hall and another locked gate at the far end, which led to the platform and the train tracks.

Inside the inspection area, hundreds of people stood in line to have their luggage inspected. The train was scheduled to depart at midnight. We waited long hours with very little to say while the tension increased. By ten o'clock, judging from the ratio of the inspectors to suitcases and bags, the likelihood of us making the train seemed slim.

When it was finally our turn, the official undid the long zippers that snaked around the enormous green duffle bags Mama had sewn, and with his grubby hands he churned through all the washed, ironed, and carefully folded sheets and clothing that we'd packed, until everything was snarled. There was something in his movements that reminded me of one horrible time in a fish store, when the salesgirl reached into a bucket of water and took out a large, live fish. She laid it on the low counter and without a thought, cut open the fish's belly and scooped out its entrails with her bare hands. Like I had then, I clung to Mama. I felt ill.

Drops of sweat appeared on Papa's forehead, like the glass beads on the forbidden necklace that was hanging around my neck. I stood waiting for the inspector's hands. He asked me to unbutton my shirt. I undid the top button, then the next one. The inspector looked as if he was about to say something. Then he changed his mind, grunted and turned to the suitcases. I was lucky. If I'd had to undo a third button he would have seen the necklace. I held my breath until he waved us on.

Our last few moments in the Soviet Union were spent trying to restore some order to our belongings so that we could cram them back into our bags. Most of the people around us on the crowded platform were doing the same. Others were hovering over their sick, elderly parents who sat forlornly on suitcases tied with string. I saw a small boy flipping through the pages of what was left of his picture book. It had been torn almost in half by the uncaring hand of the inspector. His mother wept as she smoothed out the title page of a book of poetry. It had been crumpled and ripped.

I glanced at the face of the station clock that hung on the tiled wall, and gasped. The train was leaving at midnight. In an act of deliberate malice, the gates of the inspection area had been kept closed until 11:45. When they were finally thrown open, everyone stampeded toward the train, pushing carts or dragging luggage with them. The barbed wire, the soldiers, the dogs, the chaos had put us all in a panic. Natasha and I pushed the heavy cart holding our belongings, but we made slow progress through the crowd. As we got closer to the train car, we could see that the authorities had one final cruelty in store for us. Not only were we assigned to the farthest car at the end of the train, but the platform actually stopped several meters before it reached the car's doors. It would be impossible to climb aboard without help, especially for someone as short as me.

A deep voice cut through the air. "We need the most able men and women to the front to help!"

A human chain formed spontaneously to help people breach the gap between the train steps and the platform. We could see men lifting a woman in her wheelchair up into the car. Belongings were passed from hand to hand and tossed onto the steps of the coach. But often in situations of fear and disorder, people help themselves first. As soon as people could see that their possessions were safely onboard, they clambered up after them, making it harder and harder for the rest of us, who were still standing on the platform. Soon there was nothing left of the human chain.

In the confusion, my parents and Babushka Inna found themselves on the train. Natasha and I, along with our suitcases and duffel bags, were left behind on the platform. Suddenly the platform was empty. Natasha and I were alone. The whistle blew impatiently. The train began to move, taking with it our family.

Like two mice on a wheel that turns but doesn't move forward, we tried to push our cart after the train. It was pointless. The iron serpent was too fast for us. It is hard to tell how long we ran, but suddenly, to our amazement, the train jerked, slowed down, and stopped. We had finally reached the end of the platform, but now we faced the broad gap between it and the train. Even if I could have somehow gotten down off the platform, I still wouldn't have been able to get up onto the train. My chin barely reached the bottom step.

Somehow, two railway workers materialized beside us. Natasha made sure I went first. If anyone was left behind, it wouldn't be her younger sister. One of the men picked me up and threw me through the open door. The other one helped Natasha, and then threw our suitcases after us. The bags burst open as they hit the metal stairs, scattering matrushka dolls and wooden bowls, as Mama pulled us in to safety.

It had been Papa who had tamed the beast. He had seen us running after the train when the whistle blew. He grabbed the emergency cord and pulled hard. As the train shuddered to a stop, he was surrounded by Soviet border police. In language Mama had never heard him use before, he made it clear that he was not letting go of the cord, nor was the train leaving, until his girls were onboard. His eyes burned so furiously, so wildly, that the police just stared at him. He did not let go of the cord until we were safely beside him. Only then did the train begin to roll again.

Natasha and I cried and cried in Babushka Inna's arms. She whispered into our hair, "This is the worst thing that is going to happen to you. I promise!"

A short time later, I climbed onto the top bunk and fell into a heavy, sweet sleep as the train, like a rocking cradle, carried us deep into the black inky night. I dreamed of Florence.

ACKNOWLEDGMENTS

I AM DEEPLY GRATEFUL TO MY FRIENDS WHO ENCOURAGED ME TO TELL THESE STORIES: DR. DAVID SPERLING, BARBARA FURLOW, NELLY PEREZ, AND JO ECKERLING. ADDITIONAL THANKS GO TO BRIAN Torobin and Carol Knox for their first hand in editing. I am indebted to my publisher and dear friend Kathy Lowinger, who encouraged me and helped to bring this work to life. I am grateful to Kathryn Cole and the staff at Tundra Books who courageously spent many hours somewhere between Stretskaya and Krasnapolskay Street. With love and devotion I thank my parents, Zinovy and Lana Grimberg, for their willingness to live these stories once again, and for helping me to remember – and for everything I am. With a full heart I thank my beloved Moshe, for all his support and additional hours of taking care of our son so I could write. Last but not least, I am thankful to our son, David Avracham, who always greeted me warmly despite the hours I spent away from him while working on this book. These stories are his stories. May he learn to love the people who lived them.